SECOND EDITION

THE PARENTS
BOOK OF BALLET

ANSWERS TO CRITICAL QUESTIONS ABOUT
THE CARE AND DEVELOPMENT OF THE YOUNG DANCER

SECOND EDITION

THE PARENTS
BOOK OF BALLET

ANSWERS TO CRITICAL QUESTIONS ABOUT
THE CARE AND DEVELOPMENT OF THE YOUNG DANCER

ANGELA WHITEHILL AND WILLIAM NOBLE

FOREWORD BY AMANDA MCKERROW
INTRODUCTION BY DAVID HOWARD

PRINCETON BOOK COMPANY, PUBLISHERS

A Dance Horizons Book
Princeton Book Company, Publishers
PO Box 831
Hightstown, NJ 08520-0831

Cover, interior design and composition by Lisa Denham

Library of Congress Cataloging–in–Publication Data

Whitehill, Angela

    The parents book of ballet: answers to critical questions about the
care and development of the young dancer / Angela Whitehill and
William P. Noble; introduction by David Howard. — 2nd ed.

    p. cm.
Includes bibliographical references.
ISBN 0-87127-257-1

    1. Ballet — Study and Teaching. I. Noble, William. II. Title.

GV1788.5.W48 2003

792.8'071—dc21

2003049894

Printed in The United States of America   8, 7, 6, 5, 4, 3, 2, 1

FOR AUDREY
AND IN MEMORY OF PAUL

TWO WONDERFUL PARENTS

CONTENTS

Amanda McKerrow

FOREWORD

Amanda McKerrow

Looking back on the early years of my dancing career, I realize that it must have been more stressful and worrisome for my parents than it was for me. My father was a classically–trained musician, and he had his own dance band. But he gave it up for a more stable job with the federal government because he and my mother were aware of how few people make a real living in the performing arts and that talent alone isn't enough. Yet, they were determined to give me every opportunity, including taking on the public school system where we lived because I couldn't get early school release each day to attend regular ballet classes.

Ultimately, we relocated, and I transferred to a school that was more flexible. If my parents had a resource such as this book, I'm certain it would have been much easier for them. I can't count the number of times my mother said, "I wish there was someone we could call or ask…" whether it was about pointe shoes, hair, body, school, or an audition dilemma.

Ballet is a special, beautiful, expressive art form that teaches poise, grace, discipline and self-esteem. Ballet has given me total direction in my life. I was an extremely shy and introspective child, prone to many worries. Ballet took me to a whole different world. When I was dancing, I was excited, focused and happy. Everything just felt right. One memory I will always cherish is the time my parents took me to see my first ballet performance. It was American Ballet Theatre's production of *Petrouchka* at the Kennedy Center. It was the most magical experience I ever had, and from that moment, there was never any question about my direction in life.

It takes many ingredients to make a dancer, and while the amounts may vary for each person, they are all essential. I believe these ingredients include a strong foundation, proper early training, determination, love and enthusiasm and, of course, a strong support structure consisting of family, friends and teachers. For me, it was my family. Whether driving to and from class and rehearsal, giving me a pep talk or simply being there to listen and advise, my mother, father, sister and, later, my husband have been there to support me.

One of the biggest breaks of my career may not have happened at all if it hadn't been for my wonderful family. In June, 1981, my teacher, Mary Day, took me to the Fourth International Ballet Competition in Moscow. I was only seventeen. This was the first time I would travel out of the country, and it would be for three weeks! Mary Day felt at this point in my training it would be a good experience and a great opportunity to see dancers from around the world. If I happened to take a medal, it would look great on a resumé and help me get into a company later.

With much rearranging of schedules and dipping into savings, my mother, father and sister went with me! I'm certain their love and support right there in Moscow helped give me the confidence to perform to the best of my abilities and, ultimately, to take a gold medal. Of course, a career in dance is much more than winning a medal. It is a continuation of the values learned in training as a young dancer. And while it is true the gold medal opened many doors for me, the unconditional love and support of my family has been invaluable; I don't believe I could have achieved what I have without all of them.

Trained at the Washington Ballet, at eighteen Amanda McKerrow became America's first Gold Medalist at the Moscow International Ballet Competition. She joined American Ballet Theatre in 1982 and was promoted to principal dancer in 1987. From the start, she has been a consummate professional who worked with conviction, fearlessness and high spirits. She has danced every major classical role, including Tudor's The Leaves Are Fading *and* Balanchine's Theme and Variations. *She has created roles by Tharp, De Mille, Tippet and Kudelka worldwide.*

David Howard (photo by Victor DeLiso)

INTRODUCTION

David Howard

As ballet teacher and director I understand the many questions parents and their young dancers have. I well remember my own early training in England and the bouts of confusion and uncertainty that buffeted me. Ballet training is complicated, frustrating and extremely difficult. All young dancers and their parents would not be normal if they didn't have a box full of questions for their teachers.

The real issue, however, is whether there might be answers to these questions. Ballet is an art form with a split personality — the demands on our bodies, the precision of the steps which require discipline and order... yet the training of the young dancers varies widely from school to school. My philosophy, for example, applies principles of kinesiology to dance movement and combines those with innate musicality. Others have different philosophies.

We who do the training know the answers to the questions parents put forward. But it simply doesn't occur to us that parents and their young dancers might be shy about seeking seemingly simple information such as, "How do I find a good teacher?" or "Do boys have different training than girls?" Sometimes parents aren't quite sure precisely what information they want, only that they feel a lack of hard facts, and they sense some uncertainty.

In a sense, it is a communications gap, and we must take the first step toward closing it. Our responsibility to our students requires nothing less. That is why this book is both timely and valuable. It fills a need. Parents, teachers, young dancers, even audience members, will find resources here not previously set out in such great detail, and some of the mystery of the training process will be opened up for all to see.

The process of creating a ballet dancer has been shrouded in mystery through the decades. Questions about training, auditions, schools, summer programs had no central answering service. The best authority was usually a teacher or an active artistic director. The result was a hodgepodge of information that combined personal experience with personal bias, and provided no unvarying standard. For a parent or a young dancer seeking only one simple, sure answer, it was confusing.

This book finally puts things in order, and it explains in clear words the pros and the cons of the ballet process. Choices and timing are of the utmost importance in a dancer's career. Where to study, whether and when to attend a boarding school, how to find the right teacher, how to recognize the ethical behavior of teaching principles and schools, when to go *on pointe*—these are the kinds of serious questions all parents should ask because the answers are often complex. The authors of this book take the time to show the proper way to approach such matters.

In the past thirty years ballet has spread itself more thoroughly across the face of the earth, and the result has been greater ballet interest in city after city. I see students with stronger training and background from hundreds, even thousands, of miles away. Dance has become decentralized, and this pleases me greatly because ballet is an art form for all, not just the sophisticated few. *The Parents Book of Ballet* recognizes this by offering insights from artistic directors throughout the country and by highlighting the regional ballet experience. Ballet is no longer synonymous with New York City, even though many young dancers continue to see themselves dancing with American Ballet Theatre or the New York City Ballet. These companies, however, can accommodate but 200 to 400 dancers and those applying to such companies are in the thousands. This book emphasizes that there are many excellent options available, that dancers can find a happy quality of life elsewhere, that there are fine ballet companies in such places as Atlanta, Pittsburgh, Houston, San Francisco, Dayton and Seattle.

If there is one thing I feel strongly about it is that the early development of the dancer is vitally important. Without this early training no dancer can feel the true flow of movement so necessary later on. This book will help guide parents through the joys of classical training and prepare the young dancer to the ultimate choice about a career in the world of ballet. Every responsible teacher should have a copy in their studio and make it available to aspiring dancers, and to their parents as well.

David Howard's students can be easily recognized on the stages of ballet companies great and small, in modern dance companies and on Broadway, television and in motion pictures. Among them are Mikhail Baryshnikov, Gelsey Kirkland, Natalia Makarova, Sylvie Guillem, Cynthia Harvey, Darci Kistler and Tamara Roja. He is the resident guest teacher with England's Royal Ballet and teaches at American Ballet Theatre, Steps on Broadway and Broadway Dance in New York and in Europe and Japan.

Master teacher David Howard with
Jennifer Gelfand.
(Photo by Victor DeLiso)

Creative dance classes introduce the young child to movement and music.

ONE

The best age to begin ballet

Each August the studio phone starts to ring; it's the beginning of another season, another ballet school semester. Parents are calling to enroll their children in class, and with the certainty of the season comes the frequent question:

"At what age do you start children's ballet classes?"

"Five years old for pre-ballet, seven or eight years old for regular ballet."

Sometimes there is a hush of disappointment. "My child is almost four, but she has a lovely little body. She's been dancing since she could walk."

For three or four year-olds, the physical rudiments of ballet are simply too taxing, but the demand for dance classes has become so great that many studios have designed a program which introduces the youngest children to the "sense" of ballet dance without the difficult physical demands of ballet.

"Your child could join our 'creative dance' classes," the parent is told. "It's preliminary instruction that touches on dance and music appreciation but doesn't include any formal ballet training."

Thus the process begins.

Anne Marie Rebassi, formerly an instructor with the Central Pennsylvania Youth Ballet, underscores the limits and purpose of the "creative dance" class: "At three or four, children have an extremely limited attention span, so we keep the classes to a half-hour, and we make no attempt to introduce ballet steps or terminology."

The children are shown various forms of shape and movement, items they can easily recognize, such as a butterfly, a bubble, a flower, cat or pony. They learn to beat out the syllables of their names on the floor with their hands and/or feet in a rhythmic pattern. They make shapes with their bodies—such as the letter "C" by curving their backs, or a diamond by bending their legs outward—and act out simple stories and nursery rhymes. The idea is to get them used to using their bodies in an expressive way.

"I can't wait to see my daughter in a tutu," a parent often will exclaim.

It may be a long wait. Occasionally the students may be allowed to dress up in an old costume or wear a tiara. But tutus? For their entire career dancers attend class in a solid color leotard, pink tights and ballet shoes for the girls, a white T shirt, black tights, white socks and black or white ballet shoes for the boys. Some schools have a dress code even for creative dance. Others allow a little more flexibility with leotard colors when the children are very young.

But tutus? "This isn't a ballet class," says Rebassi. "I try to teach them some classroom etiquette—how to listen and follow, not to talk, and I show them that there are different kinds of music."

Of course, there are times when parents and children are their own worst enemies...

And the first classes are not always as easy as you may hope, even when the child is destined to spend the rest of her life in the art of ballet.

At the age of three my mother took me to my first dance class. She had dreamed of becoming a dancer, but due to a family disaster, she had stopped taking classes at an early age. Now, as with so many women when they become mothers, she wanted all for me she never had. I remember the beautiful stairway that curved gracefully to the second floor studio, and I remember being filled with excitement. My mother guided me into the dressing room where the girls changed into little blue tunics and the boys into shorts. We were ushered into a huge white and gold room with two bay windows and a beautiful, shining wood floor. First, we sat on the floor and wiggled our toes; then we flexed our feet and hands; then we were told to stand.

"Now we will run around and shoot our bows," said Miss Cookearborough, the teacher.

"Oh no," I remember thinking. "I came to dance, not to shoot things!" and I stood absolutely still, and ten little children piled into me, knocking us all to the floor. I burst into tears and refused to move.

Miss Cookearborough took in the scene quickly and invited my mother to join the class instead. I was picked up and sat in a window seat to watch.

Because teaching very young children may constitute a large part of studio income, it can be hard for a teacher to refuse them admission, especially in places where the overall number of students may be small. The first step should be the creative dance experience. Occasionally, there are parents of three- and four-year-olds who won't be deterred by a refusal to teach their children formal ballet and eventually will find someone who will take their child. The consequences can be enormous: the child may be taught incorrectly, they may be hurt because of the physical demands, or may simply become bored…and the dream of a ballet career could be over before it really begins.

Proper dance instruction is based on the child's physical ability and stage of development. At four, a youngster's bones are quite soft and malleable, and severe damage could result from arduous training or exertion. Even the best and most caring teacher is not equipped to pinpoint a child's level of development at this young age—only a pediatrician could know for certain. The good ballet teacher will explain these risks to a parent.

Before enrolling your four-year-old, call the largest dance schools in the area and ask about their teaching philosophies. Do they follow a graded system? Do they give and have recitals (see Chapter Ten)? How many children are in the class? Have their students joined professional companies? At what age do students go on pointe? (If started younger than ten years old, don't consider it; see Chapter Six).

A good teacher corrects each child separately.
(Abbie Siegel, Pacific Northwest Ballet School)

Next, ask to watch a class of four-year-olds and a class of six to seven-year-olds. See how much repetition of content there is in each class; if it exists, it could go on until the child is eight or nine years old, and turn an exciting experience into a boring one. Children don't want to be flowers, trees or kittens forever…they want variety! Talk to parents of children in both classes, ask how the children have reacted, then talk to the teacher and see if she really understands the tiny child. Ask how much she expects of the creative dance class. Are they taught technique such as *barre work, arabesques* and *pirouettes?* If so, be very cautious.

Ask if the same teacher is teaching all the classes. Having different teachers over the years will be more challenging.

When the child becomes five, another level is reached. Now pre-ballet classes are appropriate, and here the children will have their first exposure to formal ballet. There are, in fact, some well-respected teachers who believe no child should even enter a dance class before the age of five because little that is taught will be retained. But the general consensus is that the creative dance experience prior to age five will encourage a child's imagination and sense of expression, regardless of what's retained, and that, certainly, will ease the transition to formal, pre-ballet training.

The beginning of a career? Pre-ballet students at Pacific Northwest Ballet School.

Two

Pre-ballet classes

A year can make such a difference! A five-year-old with a season of creative dance behind him or her must now learn to channel his sense of imagination and apply it with discipline. It is the first lesson at the beginning of a possible ballet career. Discipline…ballet is discipline; it is a close following of prescribed movements. At five years old it is time for initial exposure to the discipline, tradition and joy of pre-ballet classes.

It will be strange and exciting because it is the first real ballet class the children will experience. The class opens…and the teacher tells them to face the barre, pointing to the rounded wood or metal shape rail attached to the wall and running parallel to the floor. "Now, gently, put both your hands on it," she says.

The dancers are thrilled. Until now they haven't been allowed to touch the barre. Then, the teacher shows them two of the five ballet foot positions (the other three foot positions are more complicated and shouldn't be attempted until the children are at least eight years old), and she shows them how these should be done with a forty-five degree "turn out."

This will be their first exposure to a new ballet term. The children watch as she rotates her entire leg with the knee, calf, ankle and foot in alignment and at a forty-five degree angle to the perpendicular of her body.

Five basic foot positions. (photo by Rob Martin)

"We use turn out to make it easier to move in all directions," she says, pointing to her hip and emphasizing that everything begins from there. "Try it," she encourages, and little legs fly out unceremoniously.

Slowly, the teacher will explain a few basic warm-up exercises, showing the children how they must learn to bend. "We're trying to find our balance," she adds, and the dancers try a variety of positions. They watch her as she slowly sinks in a small half-knee bend. "We call this a *demi-plié*," she says. "See how the legs turn out. We're making a diamond shape."

As they try to follow her, she watches them carefully. It is the first ballet exercise they will learn, and she wants to make sure that, as they turn out, their knees will travel sideways and hold directly over the middle toe of the foot.

This is the only way to do a proper *demi-plié*. "Let's do some stretching," the teacher says. "Shall we be mice or snails?" The children remember that these are the exercises they learned in creative dance the year before. What they don't realize is that this role playing is essential to all dance performance.

"Now let's try to gallop across the floor…"

"Here's how we jump in first position…"

The teacher relaxes and smiles at her class. Forty-five minutes have sped by, and the five-year-olds are filled with excitement and curiosity. It has been more than enough for one day.

Without realizing it, the children have experienced the basic structure of a classical ballet class. It will not vary, no matter their age or level of accomplishment, professional dancer or limited amateur. The first pre-ballet class has established the pattern.

The idea of pre-ballet classes is not without its critics. Anne Marie Rebassi is one of these. "I don't really like to have children under the age of seven," she says, "because they are still growing physically. At seven or eight their minds and bodies begin to mesh, and this makes learning and teaching so much easier." Madeline Cantrella Culpo, artistic director of the Albany-Berkshire Ballet in Pittsfield, Massachusetts, agrees. She thinks children are starting too young. "But do we have a choice?" she asks, admitting that non-ballet dance forms such as jazz and tap will be happy to take the young child if ballet won't. "I do give pre-ballet lessons at four, but I find that four-year-olds are more sophisticated today than they were twenty years ago."

The children may enter pre-ballet classes at a young age, but that doesn't mean they will progress more quickly. "I tell every mother," Madeline Culpo says, "that I will not put her child into classical ballet classes until the child is seven. They must know the pre-ballet experience could last up to three years."

Beyond the actual ballet steps, what can a child learn in the pre-ballet years? At five and six, a child has an innocent facility to accept and remember words, names and phrases in another language, and of course the language of ballet is French. Most pick up the terminology as easily as they would learn English equivalents. At this time, too, the children are beginning to understand and feel their bodies, and they are responsive to simple correction; they *want* to learn. This is also a good time to introduce music, and to teach the child to listen and *hear* tempos and rhythms. Familiarity with all of these aspects will bridge an important gap when formal ballet classes begin.

Posture is an extremely important part of the pre-ballet class. The five– and six-year-old is only beginning to lose "baby fat" as well as his or her round little tummy, and this is the best time to teach the proper position. Correct ballet posture involves the weight held over the toes, the backs of the knees pulled up, and the thighs rotated so that the inner thigh can be seen. The lower abdominal muscles should be pulled up, the rib cage lifted but not distended, shoulders relaxed naturally, neck gracefully stretched, and the head held erect, not protruding forward.

Then the upper back will be held straight and the buttocks controlled in such a way that the spine will look like a straight line from the nape of the neck to the tail bone.

The correct ballet posture is not simple—not without arduous training—but it can be learned in pre-ballet class.

A note of caution. Many children show an interest in gymnastics at this age, and it might seem as if ballet and gymnastics would complement one another well. This is not true. Ballet can help gymnastics, especially for floor exercises, but the ballet dancer needs to maintain a straight spine. This is where the two disciplines diverge: gymnastics requires the student to curve or sway the lower back when landing, and the ballet dancer must have a strong *straight* back.

As the pre-ballet class moves along, the children will be taught a variety of steps: *relevé, battement tendu, piqué, retiré* or *passé,* and the preparation for *grand battement*. All these exercises start and finish in first position, the easiest and most familiar position for the feet to assume. Dancers, even in pre-ballet class, who can combine an understanding of these steps with the proper posture are well on their way to ballet success.

Let's not forget the arms. Ballet involves the total body, and the way the arms perform is equally as important as how the legs are seen. Pre-ballet classes get to work on the arms, too.

There are five basic arm positions, all based on a circle, each position held in front of the shoulders. Although they remain the same in every syllabus they are often numbered differently. In one syllabus a position may be called *5th*, in another *high 5th* and in yet another this same position is *3rd en haute*. It is not as confusing as it sounds and dancers quickly learn to adapt.

Three basic arm positions. (photo by Rob Martin)

Sometimes the arm positions are introduced with games and imagery, making it more fun. "I introduce a poem," says Anne Marie Rebassi, "and I have the children use their bodies and their arms to imagine the poem through dance." They move their arms in order to illustrate the poem physically, and she encourages them to *feel* the words.

As the class progresses, it is obvious the children are getting restless. Too much stationary work can be boring, especially to a five-year-old.

"Let's move over to the corner," says the teacher, and she directs them to execute some traveling steps, moving diagonally across the room. "Try to gallop like a horse," she says. "Go forward…now sideways…now back." In pairs, they make simple skips with the toe lifted to the knee, moving together, seeking a rhythm.

"Pretend there's a pool of water in the middle of the room," she says. "Let's jump over it…" and they imitate horses, up and over, legs extended, if possible. In this way she has provided the tiniest preparation, the earliest exposure to the big jumps that every ballet dancer must execute in the years ahead.

The class is over. The teacher nods at her students. In unison, the five-year-olds curtsey or bow, and the teacher smiles.

No ballet class is complete without this curtsey or bow, known as a *reverence*. Ballet is an extremely polite art, and it has a specific etiquette. To curtsey or bow is to say thank you and to show appreciation.

Learning *reverence*. (Otto Neubert, Ballet Master, Pacific Northwest Ballet)

A good teacher gives verbal and hands-on correction. (photo by Rob Martin)

THREE

Finding the right teacher

The art of ballet is a multiple discipline, combining dance movement and music with an appreciation of painting, literature, history and sculpture. The fine ballet teacher is an artist first—then a teacher, not the other way around.

The fine ballet teacher infuses a child with a deep love of all the arts and must have a personal respect and love for the ballet art form. The teacher should believe in it and live it.

Parents must search out the teacher's background, and the key is to determine if the teacher has a minimum of six to ten years of training with a recognized and reliable ballet school, or degree in dance from a recognized college or university dance program. There are a few institutions such as Virginia Intermont College, University of Hartford (Connecticut) and University of Utah that provide excellent training for those who will eventually teach ballet. Of course, a ballet school attached to a recognized professional ballet company such as the San Francisco Ballet, the Pacific Northwest Ballet in Seattle or the New York City, Boston and Cincinnati Ballet companies can provide strong training. Outside the United States, the London School of the Arts Education Trust or one of the many technical arts schools in the United Kingdom and the Vaganova Institute in St. Petersburg (Russia) offer superior opportunities for those who will teach ballet.

While professional stage experience is not mandatory, it is certainly helpful. But note this: there are many fine teachers who have not danced professionally; a teacher with careful training and no professional experience is far preferable to one with extensive stage experience and poor training.

What if the teacher teaches many dance forms (such as jazz, modern and ballet)? Be careful. Most highly–qualified ballet teachers limit themselves to ballet only. If the studio offers other dance forms, be sure other qualified teachers will teach them. The ballet art form is too highly specialized and too demanding for a teacher to mix her ballet discipline with other dance techniques.

An important consideration must be the *instructional syllabus* that the teacher and the school will follow. Parents should become familiar with the overall plan (a more detailed discussion of the syllabus can be found in Chapter Five). There are a number of recognized syllabuses, all based on Russian, French, English, Danish or Italian ballet traditions, and any one of them would be appropriate. The syllabus is the actual plan of instruction: the number of classes per day and week, the movements to be learned and followed, body emphasis (in Russia, for example, the system trains particularly strong and muscular dancers) and the yearly progression of skills. The syllabus should take the child from the point of entry into the ballet world to the pre-professional level, a period of at least eight to ten years.

Classical ballet was formalized by Louis XIV of France who created the *Academie Royale de Danse* in 1661 in Paris, and because of this all ballet terms have remained French. The art developed in other European countries as well, and with it certain definable ballet traditions. For example, in Italy, Enrico Cecchetti created a beautiful system which emphasizes the *port-de-bras* (carriage of the arms and body); while in England, Adeline Genée created the Royal Academy of Dancing, which established an exacting grade system for dancers starting at age six and continuing to age eighteen.

These and other recognized European systems are taught in the United States, and they are excellent instructional plans. In particular, the Cecchetti and Royal Academy of Dancing systems offer yearly refresher courses for teachers as well as examinations for students. These latter, because of their wide acceptance, provide worthwhile national and international evaluation levels so students, no matter their location, can be judged fairly and accurately. "The beauty of the (RAD) system," says Alun Jones, former artistic director of Louisville Ballet in Kentucky, "is that they are constantly updating their class–work and syllabus."

What, then, might an appropriate examination syllabus contain? It will include barre and center work, some simple variations and, sometimes, mime and character dancing. Because the work is predetermined, some of the examination can become a bit tedious. A truly talented ballet teacher will prepare her students with a mixture of syllabus work and other aspects of technique, including—in the higher grades—some performance and repertoire.

The syllabus is the key to everything. Some fine teachers do not wish to adhere to the rigid demands of a pre-conceived syllabus, preferring instead to follow their own designs. There is nothing wrong with this, provided they have a sound knowledge of existing systems (including the Vaganova system from Russia, the Bournonville system from Denmark, as well as the Cecchetti and Royal Academy of Dancing systems), and they provide a sound grading system. This can have a happy effect on the child because the teacher represents a varied learning history that comprises the best of everything. The important thing is to ask!

When considering a school or studio, ask at what age is the child allowed to begin dancing "on pointe." Any school that starts them before the age of nine or ten should *not* be considered. Why? It's a case of the willing mind and the unwilling body. Children may think they are ready to go on pointe, but a young child's bones are soft and malleable, and long-lasting damage can occur in the legs and back if the body isn't ready for the heavy pointe demands (for a thorough discussion of "pointe" work, see Chapter Six). The first two or three years of syllabus work are carefully designed to teach the child the correct use of muscles and body placement which will prepare them for dancing on the toes.

There are, of course, exceptional children who can start this training early. But these are few, and most good ballet teachers carry a built-in skepticism about them. Six- or seven-year-olds are too young! Period!

Unfortunately, there is no licensing requirement for dance teachers, and while the profession has tried self-policing, it has met with indifferent results. Some dance teacher organizations examine teachers for membership, but they are not especially geared for ballet.

IS THERE A RIGHT TEACHER FOR EVERYONE? ABSOLUTELY.

A good way to choose a teacher and a school is to ask questions and to follow the steps outlined below. Visit the school and watch a class. The teacher should be giving verbal and "hands-on" corrections; class should be disciplined. Do not choose a teacher because of location, price or convenience! Ease of car–pooling or allowing a child to be with her best friend in class are *not* reasons to choose either a teacher or a school. Improper training can result in malformed bones, improper muscle structure and career frustration. Ballet training is serious training, and it should be approached in a serious manner.

Finding the teacher isn't hard when you know what to look for. She or he should

- Be an artist, first.
- Have strong training fundamentals.
- Have a well–disciplined approach to students.

• Follow a carefully designed syllabus of instruction.

And you shouldn't stop here. Although there are many fine teachers who fit these requirements and who will train the child correctly, there are others who might do an even better job. These are the teachers who truly love their art and truly love their students…and fit all of the above characteristics!

Victoria Pulkkinen teaching the barre stretch. (Pacific Northwest Ballet School)

You will know them by the way they hold their students' rapt attention, by the enthusiastic way they speak of their work and by the sensitive way they deliver their lessons. The right teacher is simply this: someone completely engrossed in teaching and the well-being of the students.

Reading about ballet is a wonderful way to help a child,
and the parent, to understand the art.
(photo by Rob Martin)

FOUR

Ballet outside the studio

"You could tell that ballet was her life," says a principal dancer with the New York City Ballet, referring to Alexandra Danilova, who always came to class in a matching outfit and perfume. "She was so feminine."

Ballet was her life, her central motivator, her consuming passion. The extraneous pieces of her existence could come together when ballet was involved. Her life and her art became one.

Ballet is not a dance discipline that should be left within the walls of the studio. It needs expression in the steps of our daily lives. The more attention it is paid here, the more creative and effective it will be elsewhere. Ballet, to the dance professional, is a *way* of life, and the studio is only one place where it is practiced.

When Eddy Toussaint was Artistic Director of Ballet de Montreal, he always said, "My dancers must be princesses and princes outside the studio as well as inside. Ballet was created for the royal court, and it's a regal art. No chewing gum and tee shirts on the street. Not for my dancers!"

No one expects our young children to embrace this level of dedication, nor should they try to understand its effect. There is, however, something in this portrait of deportment that should have meaning—even for the beginning dancer.

Ballet is a *creative* art. Children love to be exposed to it in its various forms. Watching the movie "The Turning Point," or even "Barbie Nutcracker" shows an aspect of the art that the regular Tuesday afternoon class couldn't show. Wouldn't a trip to a museum to look at the paintings and sculpture of Edgar Degas provide insights barre work couldn't offer? Creativity is stimulated this way; it makes the studio work more meaningful. One never knows what will take a young person's fancy.

> *I took my three-year-old son to see the Pennsylvania Ballet's version of* The Nutcracker. *A friend was dancing the Chinese variation, and she had promised to stay in costume after the performance for my son. We arrived at the theater just as the lights dimmed, and a white spotlight played on the conductor mounting the podium. My son's eyes grew huge as he watched the baton come down for the first note, and they stayed transfixed throughout the performance. Never once did he watch the dancing! Afterwards, we went backstage, and my son rushed up to my friend. "Can I meet the 'ductor?" he asked, ignoring her elaborate costume. For the next year he walked around with a stick in his hand proclaiming a future career.*

The Nutcracker is probably the single most stimulating ballet experience any young child can have. Between 500 and 800 professional companies

The Nutcracker may be the first ballet a child will see.
(Pacific Northwest Ballet)

offer this beloved classic in live performances throughout the United States each year, with many ballet schools and junior ballet companies also presenting the work. It is a Christmas pageant that every young ballet dancer will yearn to be a part of.

The story is a fairy tale and can have a cast of 100 or more. As a member of the audience, the young dancer will start to grasp the connection between the studio and the stage. There is something for everyone in this ballet, from the magical snowfall to sensuous Arabian dancers, from exciting Russian folk dancing to the Sugar Plum Fairy and her Cavalier, and finally from the fun of the battle with The Mouse King to the sheer beauty of classical ballet. In many productions, the lead female, Clara (called Maria in some versions), and her Nutcracker Prince fly in and out of the Kingdom of the Sweets in a balloon or ride on the back of a magic swan or in a sleigh.

The rich fantasy of *The Nutcracker* enlivens a child's sense of imagination, and this, in turn, feeds a budding creativity. Prepare the beginning dancer for the experience, and the results could be exciting! Read the E. T. Hoffman classic to your child, making sure it is one of the modern versions which relates directly to the ballet.

Once a live performance of *The Nutcracker* has been seen, seek out the American Ballet Theatre's video version starring Mikhail Baryshnikov and Gelsey Kirkland. The youngster can experience the thrill of pretending she or he is on stage, understanding now that this is the ultimate goal for all ballet performers.

Books also help. Your local Borders or Barnes & Noble should have a section of dance titles and publishers. Princeton Book Company has a free catalogue of books and video titles, many of which would be useful. Many books show ballet technique in words and pictures which can be read and explained to the beginning dancer. Among the easiest to grasp are:

1st, 2nd, 3rd and 4th Steps in Classical Ballet
by Thalia Mara, recently reissued by Dance
Horizons/Princeton Book Company, Publishers.

The Royal Book of Ballet, by Shirley Goulden (Follet).
This is a beautifully illustrated book which tells the stories
of the most beloved ballets.

Ballet Shoes by Noel Streatfield (Random House Children's
Books). The story of three twentieth–century children and their
journey into the ballet world.

Angelina Ballerina (Pleasant Corporation, Publishers).
A series about a dancing mouse.

How well does reading work? Melissa Sondrini, who became a principal
dancer with the Hartford (Connecticut) Ballet, remembers her
beginning years: "When I was young, my mom kept my interest in dance
through books—she never had to push me into ballet." There were other
pulls on her time such as swimming and being with friends who didn't
share her interest in dance. But the books were there for her to read
and enjoy if she wanted, and there was never pressure to commit to
ballet. "It was always up to me if I wanted to do one thing more than
another." When she wasn't in dance class, she read and read and gradually
her dedication to ballet grew until she reached the age of fifteen. Then
she decided to make ballet her career. "There was really nothing else
that interested me as much as dance," she said. For Melissa, ballet became
a way of life.

Television and video can play an important part in enlarging the
beginning dancer's horizons. Public television (PBS) and the A&E and
Bravo cable networks often present performances by some of the world's
greatest ballet companies, and young dancers should be encouraged to
watch. "Look!" a parent can point out. "That's the kind of *jeté* you are
learning," or "See how she looks so much like a swan." Video taping

those productions will allow parent and child to enjoy the performances over and over.

Search out videos or DVDs of ballet stories such as *Swan Lake, Sleeping Beauty* or *Cinderella*. Read these beloved classics and then <u>show</u> your child the ballet. As tiny dancers grow they can then compare different companies dancing the same ballets and learn much about the art. Princeton Book Company and Kultur have many video offerings such as Pacific Northwest Ballet's Maurice Sendak-designed *Nutcracker* or *Swan Lake* danced by the Royal Ballet, the Kirov or American Ballet Theatre.

Among other commercial videos, one of the most useful and entertaining is "The Children of Theatre Street" (Kultur), a documentary about the training of children at the Kirov School in Russia. The lucky ones graduate into the world-famous Kirov Ballet, and for the beginning dancer it is important to see that what they are being asked to do in class in America is hardly different from what Russian children are doing in their classes. The fact that the ultimate payoff may be as a company member in the Kirov Ballet won't be lost on many.

An important part of a child's training must include music and its relationship to the dance and dancer. It is here that you can help your child with the gift of music, piano, flute or violin classes, a good quality sound system and exposure to classical music. Introduce compact disks with music by Tchaikovsky, Berlioz, Gottschalk, Debussy, Glazunov, or Prokofiev's *Peter and the Wolf* (narrated by Peter Ustinov or Leonard Bernstein) or *Carnival of the Animals* by Saint Saëns. A luxury for the young dancer is the chance to find a private place, turn on the music and just dance!

As birthdays and other gift–giving events come around, the choices are limitless. For the very young child, there are bears and dolls dressed in tutus, or maybe a tiny "tutu" from the local dance shop (not, of course, a genuine tutu which may cost thousands of dollars!), a small pair of ballet slippers to hang on the wall, or posters and books. As the dancer grows older there are ballet bags, hair ornaments, chiffon skirts, pretty leotards, unitards and pointe shoe accessories and, for the older dancer, a signed photograph of a favorite prima ballerina or premier danseur, a trip to New York City to see a performance or a class with a master teacher.

Underlying all of this is the fact that ballet is but one kind of dance and that all dance forms have the expression of movement in common. For the beginning dancer it is important to remember that folk dancing, for instance, or square dancing and even clogging are also expressions. Dance is a social event. People enjoy doing it and watching it together. It is not just arduous studio exercise.

For the young dancer, then, ballet may not yet be a way of life, but it lives outside the studio walls, and the parent who encourages this perception will find ample rewards as the dancer's skills burgeon inside the studio.

The barre *port de bras*. (Pacific Northwest Ballet School)

Learning the children's ballet syllabus

Every school of ballet and every teacher of ballet should have a *plan of instruction* called a syllabus. It is the essential ingredient in all ballet instruction. This plan of instruction operates from the first day an excited four-year-old enters the studio and carries forward, week after week, month after month, year after year, until an accomplished seventeen or eighteen year–old proudly exhibits his or her first company contract. The syllabus informs the teacher and student, parent and director what has been learned, what will be learned, when and how. It is a road map of lesson plans that will take undeveloped talent and turn it into graceful, expressive ballet years into the future.

Every ballet parent and student should be familiar with the syllabus the teacher follows. There should be no surprises, no uncertainties.

We start with *self-discipline*. Ballet class means self-discipline! It means attending class day after day through each level of instruction. It means giving up certain pleasures such as a best friend's birthday party or a quick visit to grandmother, listening and following the teacher, being serious about the art.

Agnes de Mille, a great twentieth–century American choreographer, writes: "Never miss the daily practice, hell or high water, sickness or health. Never miss the barre practice. Miss meals, sleep, rehearsal even, but not the practice, not for one day, ever, under any circumstances…"

Tough stuff for an eight-year-old, perhaps, but the principle is clear: self-discipline is what should drive the young dancer. For the parent, the important thing is to realize that as the child grows, the demands for self-discipline will become encompassing, more insistent. The young dancer's ballet school syllabus will be founded upon it.

From the first day of ballet training (following the creative dance and pre-ballet experiences), class follows a definite format. This will usually not vary no matter who the teacher, the school or the level of training. Class always begins with exercises at the barre, then continues with stretching. Then follows a *adagio, pirouettes, petit allegros, grand allegros* and fast turns and jumps. The normal class lasts from an hour to an hour-and-a-half and concludes with a bow or curtsey (called a *reverence*).

Eight-year-olds certainly can't perform all these movements, and the appropriate ballet syllabus takes that into account. Classes are structured so that learning each movement can be the success point the children strive for.

There are a number of basic ballet syllabuses, some more prominent in Europe, some more closely followed in the United States. Most are excellent because they have stood the test of time, developing ballet dancers through the decades and providing rigid standards by which to judge the art and its practitioners. Among the more notable syllabuses used in the United States are the Royal Academy of Dancing and British Ballet Organization (British), Cecchetti (Italian) and Vaganova (Russian). All teach not only ballet steps but also the rules of ballet, such as the correct positions of the head, arms, legs and feet and direction of the body in relation to the studio or stage. The different systems do use some different terms. The names of the arm positions vary but the actual shape and execution of the movements do not.

Ballet is much more than a basic routine of dance steps. It is a full artistic experience. Bruce Marks, former artistic director of the Boston Ballet, is adamant on this point, and he feels that a concentration on the mechanics of ballet at the expense of a broader artistic purpose is ultimately harmful. "Often a dancer can do well in class, but it doesn't mean that dancer can dance; it means the dancer can do ballet class," he says. "I find more and more that these classes do not relate to what we do on stage." For Marks the important thing is to teach students how to perform, not how to take a ballet class.

Yet, if the syllabus is closely followed, a creative teacher will adapt those portions she or he thinks are most useful and discard those that might not be appropriate. For example, Noble Barker, former director of the New Haven (CT) School of Ballet, says that the Vaganova syllabus "relates the work to what is done on stage" and that is fine for some dancers, but not for all. "The students who are really good get great, the students in the middle get hurt," he insists. "There are a lot of kids out there that who have enough ability, but they get discouraged by the forced turnout and all the *relevé*. So I just use the things I think are important."

There is certain logic in the order that ballet movement is taught, and each syllabus stresses that progression. Some of the more common movements and the years in which they should be tried include:

FIRST YEAR

- simplified combinations of the basic exercises, such as *demi-plié* in first, second, third positions.
- barre work, such as *dégagé, ronde de jambe, passé,* preparation for *"grand battement,"* all with emphasis on proper body placement, very important here because bad habits picked up now could be impossible to correct later on.
- simple stretching exercises off the barre which can be carefully practiced at home so muscles can maintain suppleness.

- once stretching exercises finish, the *port-de-bras* are taught with use of head, eyes and upper body for all five positions. In the center (center work), the dancers learn simple steps such as preparation for *pirouettes, gallops,* skips, slides *(glissade)* jumps *(sauté).*
- in the British syllabus, a simple dance and some introduction to mime and simple rythms are taught.

After barre exercises, dancers stretch.
(Pacific Northwest Ballet School)

SECOND YEAR

More difficult steps are added including but not limited to:

- *grand plié* at the barre.
- simple *developé* at 45%, *battement frappé*, full *grand battement.*
- in the center, simple *adagios* and *pirouettes.*
- more complicated *ports de bras, chassé, jeté, pas de basque, piqué* turns across the floor.
- simple *grand jeté.*

Bruce Wells teaches *port de bras* at an audition class.
(Pacific Northwest Ballet School)

THIRD YEAR

- 90 degree turnout of legs and feet, fifth position.
- more complicated jumps, *pirouettes.*
- head movements with *adagio.*
- beginning beaten steps, turning steps in the air, *piqué* turns across the floor.

FOURTH AND FIFTH YEARS

By this time a young dancer should have a full working vocabulary of steps and should be able to turn and beat all the steps that require turning and beating, pointe work, classical variations and beginning partnering.

Center work is part of every class. (photo by Rob Martin)

Other movements such as multiple *pirouettes,* waltzes, moving steps, gallops and big jumps follow along during these initial years, but each has its place in the syllabus and will not be explored until the young dancer is prepared. It is interesting to note, though, that ballet tradition has established these movements in a proper logical sense of order.

Marcia Dale Weary, artistic director of the Central Pennsylvania Youth Ballet says, "I usually teach pirouettes from second position [feet approximately eighteen inches apart, sideways]. Someone once said, 'Why don't you try that from fourth or fifth position [one foot in front of the other]?' It seemed like a good idea so I tried it, but it just didn't work. Second position is best for pirouettes because the students can feel themselves springing up and bringing their leg in better."

No parent, without a prior dance career, could be expected to know and understand the many details in a ballet syllabus. Nor is it necessary.

A good teacher should be able to point to the syllabus he or she is following and to interpret it properly so young dancers will have a firm, valuable grounding in the art. Parents should be able to rely on the teacher for this.

There are, however, certain things a parent can do that will help a budding ballet career. The esoteric aspects of a syllabus notwithstanding, parents should be watchful to make sure that the craft of ballet is being taught:

- Are the legs and feet being forced to turn out? Are the knees in line with the toes?
- Are the children being made to listen carefully to the music? They should develop their sense of musicality now because it is important in later years.

The pre-teen years are probably the most important in a dancer's training. It is between the ages of eight through twelve that the basics of ballet are learned, and these will form the foundation for an ultimate professional career. Attention, discipline, careful execution and a good ballet teacher are what it will take. Parents have to be involved because young dancers need extraordinary guidance as they immerse themselves in this encompassing art form.

"My parents were so careful in selecting how I would train," says American Ballet Theatre prima ballerina Amanda McKerrow. "My mother read a great deal before placing me in a Royal Academy of Dance school, and once I had completed all the examinations, she switched me to a school that taught the Vaganova system. The combination of the two gave me purity of line and incredible strength."

A parent who understands the value of a ballet syllabus will be a participant in the young dancer's blossoming career.

Dancers start pointe work holding on to the barre, both feet on the ground.
(photo by Rob Martin)

SIX

Going on pointe—how and why

If a lovely sound is one mark of a songbird, then unadorned grace is one mark—for some, *the* mark—of an accomplished ballet dancer. Grace, above all, because it presents beauty and style and elegance with seeming effortlessness, spurring the art form to ever–higher accomplishment. Grace is sought in movement, in stage presence, in costuming, in total performance. And what is lovelier than a graceful body fully extended and balanced confidently on a tiny point of the toe? It is symmetry, charming in color and shape with perfect proportions of beauty and skill: the dancer on pointe.

Dancing on pointe is not easy to learn and even more difficult to master, but essential for the young ballet dancer. Most classical ballet work requires some dancing on pointe. It is as much a part of the ballet dancer's training and repertoire as an *arabesque* or a *port de bras.*

There is no *right age* to start. It depends on the teacher, the syllabus, the child's development and physical readiness. Children have "green bones" which can be compared to the soft and malleable young willow. Bones in the feet, legs and back can be injured by premature pointe work. The teacher must be allowed to make the decision (and be held responsible for it) when the child is ready to begin pointe work.

Only girls dance on pointe. Boys rarely do. One reason is that female musculature develops differently; the male body is built in such a way that pointe work is almost impossible. The choreography of ballet calls for the female to dance on pointe, it helps to define the ethereal quality of the character being portrayed and the otherworldliness of the dancer.

To dance on pointe is a dancer's rite of passage to advanced status as any other thing in her ballet training.

Once the young dancer is ready for pointe work, the serious business of ballet has really begun. A good teacher will look for:

- strong feet
- a graceful line from ankle to toe
- the toe pointed, not curled, when stretched
- the use of muscles on top of the foot as well as on the arches
- straight and strong legs, knees and thighs in proper alignment
- the satorious muscle (inner thigh) visible and well–developed when the dancer is in *relevé* or sitting on the floor, legs apart and stretching
- a straight spine
- strong abdominal muscles
- a full understanding of correct body placement.

Generally, the first exposure to pointe work will not come until the latter part of the second or third training year when the students have been developing along a constant, well-structured path. Careful preparation is so important.

Initial exercises will last from five to ten minutes, and they are usually given at the end of class because they represent a major departure from anything learned before. They are hard to do and they sometimes hurt! They should be taught holding onto the barre, both feet on the ground.

One major problem: because the early pointe work is introduced near the end of the year, many young dancers take it upon themselves to practice, practice, practice during the summer. *This is not a good idea* unless there is expert supervision handy. The reason? Practice without direction can be injurious, even dangerous. Without sufficient knowledge the young dancer is unable to make the proper body and placement corrections, and should she escape injury, there is a real risk of learning improper movements that must be unlearned when she resumes classes in the fall, assuming she hasn't already developed muscle habits that might be impossible to redirect.

The key to pointe work is proper pointe shoes (see the next chapter for a thorough discussion). The teacher should be the main guide, and once the shoes have been bought, the teacher should check the fit carefully. A snug fit is essential. Anything less can bring toe blisters and possible sprained ankles, a pulled ligament or tendon.

Pointe shoes must not be bought with an eye toward the child's future growth. Pointe shoes must be fitted for now, not a month or two from now. If they are to be used, they must fit the moment.

The pointe shoe, when properly worn, is secured by ribbons that circle the ankle and lower leg. These ribbons are not part of the shoe when it is bought, and many teachers ask that parents avoid sewing on the ribbons for their child. "Learning to sew the ribbon on the shoe is an integral part of the training," says one well-known teacher. "Every dancer – the famous as well as the beginner – has her own special way to prepare her shoe; it becomes a personal ritual." It is part of the teacher's curriculum to teach the dancer how to prepare her shoes.

The initial pointe class, therefore, resembles less an hour of dance instruction and more a period of manual arts. "Bring a needle, heavy duty cotton thread, scissors, ribbons and elastic," the teacher will say. "We're going to learn to prepare our pointe shoes."

Slowly, the work proceeds, and finally the shoes are adorned and fitted. "Slip them on," the teacher says. "Be sure they feel snug." There is joy on every face.

It takes many months of work before the dancer
performs an arabesque on pointe.
(photo by Ralph J. Carbo, Jr.)

When my daughter was ten years old, she and her ballet class were allowed to buy their first pointe shoes. A local shoe store brought dozens of pairs to the studio, and as each child was fitted, she dashed home joyfully, clutching the precious pink satin shoes.

Finally, only my daughter, the salesman and I were left in the studio. None of the new shoes fitted my daughter's narrow foot. Tears in her eyes, and the salesman shook his head sadly. Then I remembered there were pointe shoes in the costume shop. A friend had given them to me when his store went out of business.

We found them, stained from age, but unused. My daughter slipped them on, and the fit was perfect. A beautiful smile replaced the tears. She took my hand, rose on pointe, unsteadily, to be sure, and, to my horror, ran out of the studio, across the lawn and into the house.

To show Dad. "I'm on pointe," she told him, her little legs wobbly and insecure.

For the first few months, the major pointe exercises will be at the barre, holding on with both hands and practicing *relevés* (slow rises through the ball of the foot onto the tip of the toe) in four of the five basic positions (1st, 2nd, 4th and 5th). Only after the young dancer is able to roll slowly on and off pointe with her whole foot, similar to the way she uses her feet in *battement tendu* can the next progression be tried, a *relevé* on one foot. Then additional progressions will be added, as each prior one is mastered: *echappés, temps liés, piqués,* and finally the *bourée.*

Body placement is an important part of the dancer's training.
(photo by Angela Whitehill)

Anyone doubting that pointe work can be excruciatingly difficult needs only to hear Lupe Serano, one of the foremost ballerinas in the United States. She calls the *bourée* "the hardest step ever invented," saying she would rather "do thirty-two *fouettés* or a series of *entrechat-six* than *bourée* across the stage."

All of that is far in the future of the young dancer. In the first year it is unlikely any pointe work will take place without the barre. If the teacher does take her student off the barre, it will be for simple *boureés* and *sousous* with both feet securely on the ground. No one-footed steps yet.

In the second year, more complicated steps at the barre will be practiced, and preparations for *pirouettes* and *balancés* can be started.

Pointe work can't be rushed. It is too difficult and demanding to expect immediate skill. True ballet grace is only achieved through constant work and training, and as with other beautiful art forms, what we see as spectators is the culmination of arduous effort, extensive learning, and talent honed through dedication and patience.

"She is so graceful," we may say, as the lovely ballerina glides on pointe across the stage.

But it isn't easy.

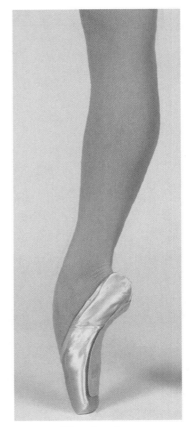

The pointe shoe.
(photo by Paul B. Goode)

All about pointe shoes

A mother's first reaction: "My God! You'll ruin your feet."

"Oh, Mother!" The young dancer shakes her head. "All ballet dancers wear pointe shoes."

The mother grimaces. "Such little support along the sides and such narrow soles! I don't see how they hold you up."

The truth is the pointe shoe does its job well and efficiently, even if it looks like it couldn't support a wraith. Hard, square toe, soft sides, ribbon and elastic that drawn tight can cut off circulation, an unforgiving, narrow sole. A former student used to call them "pretty pink satin torture chambers."

Dancing on pointe has a long history, and the first shoes were probably designed so the dancer could surpass the tiptoe grace that even modest training might achieve. If the dancer could truly rise to the pinnacle of her foot, the body could become an unbroken line, an element of perfection, throughout.

The pointe shoe dates back at least 200 years to the time of Marie Taglioni, whose early nineteenth century performances were the toast of Europe. Ballet lore says that she was the first to rise on pointe (some historians say that others preceded her) though there is doubt that she actually danced in this position. More likely, she posed on pointe, returning to the usual flat position when movement was required. Her original pointe shoes have been preserved, and it's obvious they were not designed for demanding choreography. They were simply not sturdy enough.

Even if Taglioni was the first to rise on pointe, the practice was not uniformly adopted. It took years before the *corps de ballet* would follow along, and it took still more years before the *corps* would dance, rather than pose, on pointe.

Now, of course, dancing on pointe is an integral part of any dancer's training, and through generations the pointe shoe has been transformed into a marvelously precise instrument. The correct shoe can work wonders for the dancer. It is as much a part of her art as an exquisite *arabesque* or a soaring *grand jeté*.

But what of the pointe shoe? What should we know? To start with, the following terms should be understood:

Paste Shoe The traditional pointe shoe.

New Materials Shoe Pointe shoes made with synthetic box and/or shanks.

Box The stiffened part of the shoe that encases the toe.

Pointe The art of rising to the tip of the toe.

Vamp The part of the box from the top of the toes to the underside where pleating meets sole.

Shank The inner sole.

Pleating The satin drawn over the front of the toe and folded under the toe where it is joined to the sole.

Darning Embroidering the tip of the toe and the pleats with silk thread.

Ribbons One–half–inch wide satin pieces attached to the shoe with a grosgrain or rougher texture on the reverse side.

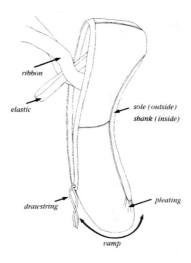

ribbon

elastic

sole (outside)
shank (inside)

drawstring

pleating

vamp

Parts of the pointe shoe.

The shoe Marie Taglioni wore so many years ago had no hardened box (thus making it difficult to rise on pointe). It had flexible leather soles (thus making it difficult to hold balance on pointe), silk satin tops and darning along the sides and under the pointe (thus increasing the sturdiness of the over-all shoe, but not the pointe area). It's obvious she could not have stayed on pointe long.

A certain myth exists that pointe shoes have wood or steel in the toes. Nothing could be less true. Much of the construction of pointe shoes is done by master cobblers following generations-old techniques. The top of the shoe is made of layers of canvas and satin (great ballerinas such as Margot Fonteyn of London's Royal Ballet had the top layer made from pure silk because it was more sturdy and less slippery than synthetic satin). The upper part of the shoe–made of satin–wraps around and under the foot and is attached to a stiff, narrow sole, and the cobbler uses a special tool to pleat the satin before sewing it to the sole because there cannot be any bumpy or ragged edges in the satin which could throw off the dancer's balance.

On top, the many layers of canvas are glued together to create the box, and a drawstring runs around the outer edge of the shoe so that the dancer can adjust it to fit her foot snuggly and comfortably. It is the box that the dancer rises onto when going on pointe, and if there is any uncertainty in the fit, the pointe position will disintegrate.

What shoe to buy, then? The teacher is the first person ask.

Most importantly, there is a correct shoe for every dancer *but it may differ from dancer to dancer!* Not everyone should wear the same kind of shoe.

Why? Because the shoe type depends on the structure of the dancer's foot, and some types of shoes are more appropriate for one configuration, other types for another. Certain shoe brands offer special characteristics. Over the past few years there have been many new pointe shoes introduced. Of the thirty companies and many styles, most readily available and popular are:

> *Bloch:* an Australian shoe that comes in twelve styles, many of which can be ordered with a specific shank strength.
>
> *Capezio:* the most available shoe in the United States, this company builds shoes not only for professional dancers but for the beginner in all types of studio training. Available in eleven styles and a variety of widths and colors.
>
> *Freed of London:* used by many of the great professional dancers, this British shoe has an easy break in period and comes in four styles in four widths. All shoes are handmade and the company does its best to ensure specific "makers" but they don't last very long.

Chacotte: a subsidiary of Freed of London, this shoe can be specially ordered or purchased in two models, four widths and two shanks. Known for a short break-in period.

Gamba: available through Repetto retailers, this shoe comes in eight styles including the ABT model which was designed for students at American Ballet Theatre.

Gaynor Minden: designed and manufactured by an ex-dancer, it uses synthetics in the shanks which not only extend the durability and reduce the break-in period but insure consistency. They are available in three widths, vamps and box styles, five shanks and four heel heights. They are readily available and are the biggest breakthrough in pointe shoes in many years.

Grishko: a Russian shoe in eight styles. These are created by cobblers from the Bolshoi and Kirov Ballet Companies and are designed to accommodate the Russian technique as well as the Elevé models which are quiet and pliable.

Prima Soft: offering five models, these shoes also are designed by an ex–dancer and use synthetics to increase life and reduce break–in time. This shoe has "graduated memory shanks" which allow the shoe to restore its shape when the dancer stands flat.

Sansha: offering nine models and four widths, this shoe is famed for its replaceable shank system which allows the dancer to lengthen or shorten the shank as needed.

In addition to these companies and their shoe styles, others can be found by clicking on the Internet and going to available Web sites. Some notables include:

American:

    Danshuz/Style Queen: www.dancingwithstyle.com
    Freddy: www.freddy.com
    Fuzi International: www.fuzi.net
    Karl-Heinz Martin: www.evapointeshoes.com
    Leo's: www.leosdancewear.com

Liberts: www.liberts.com

Russian Pointe: www.russianpointe.com

So'Danca: www.sodanca.com

Canadian:

Angelo Luzio: www.angeloluzio.com

Principal Pointe Shoes: www.pagesshoeroom.com

Russian:

Petrushka and Rusbai: www.petrushka-ballet.com

Vozrozhdenia: vozroz@mail.wplus.net

English:

Dance Workshop 2000: www.danceworkshop2000.com

Japanese:

Sylvia: www.sylvia.co.jp

Italian:

Porselli: www.teatro-danza.it/porselli

A few companies do not have Web sites at time of writing, but their telephone numbers follow:

Australian:

Salvio: 011-61-02-0398 3502

Austrian:

Schachtner: 800-762 0789

French:

Merlet: 011-33-555-38-87-78

Repetto: 800-858-5855

Mexican:

    Miguelito: 210-349-2573

South African:

    Teplov: 011-27-21-854-6928

The shoes are chosen and bought. Next comes customizing.

Professional dancers take the basic pointe shoe and have it customized to suit their own designs. They might:

- Cut down on the box size or extend the vamp.
- Cut down the shoe sides because it can enhance the look of the pointed foot.
- Have the heels cut up higher so the shoe won't slip off.
- Have a lighter sole or a shorter shank.

Customizing one's shoes means that every pair has to be especially ordered from the manufacturer. For the young student dancer this may mean added expense and the possibility that significant time delays might affect class time and proper training. Even for professionals this can mean problems:

Some time ago I decided to take a year off from dancing and worked with the Atlanta Ballet as costumer. One dancer insisted on special-order Gamba shoes from England.

I had ordered them for her in August and by the first performance of Nutcracker—*in November—they still hadn't arrived. Numerous phone calls to the Gamba store in London had proved unavailing. Finally, I tried to find her a close substitute even as we began touring. In airport after airport I called local and national shoe suppliers, but there was nothing suitable. First, she would dance in one brand, then another, never comfortable, never settled. And, of course, her dancing suffered because her feet hurt.*

Then, with only six performances left, the Gamba shoes arrived. Joyfully, she put them on and started to dance—only to wither in pain because her feet no longer found them compatible. The other shoe varieties had changed her technique.

Most young dancers do not special order shoes but customize them themselves.

A mother's reaction:

"You're destroying that beautiful shoe!"

"Oh, Mom! I'm breaking them in."

The back center seam is pushed down inside the sole.

"It's ripping!"

Needle and thread in hand, the young dancer begins to sew a piece of ribbon onto the side of the shoe fold. "That's not ordinary thread!"

"It's heavy duty cotton," the young dancer says. "Some people use dental floss."

"Ugh!"

"The ribbon's important. It wraps around our ankles and gives support when we're on pointe."

Pieces of elastic, about three-quarters of an inch wide, are attached to the back of the shoe. The young dancer slips her foot under the elastic so it is stretched over her instep.

"Won't that stop your blood circulation?"

"It's so my shoe doesn't slip off."

The mother picks up the other shoe and examines the toe point. There's heavy darning about an inch square on the tip of the toe.

"What is this for?"

"My pointe work. It's like a cushion, and it prevents slipping when I'm working on a wooden floor. My teacher taught us how to do it with embroidery thread."

Although some teachers don't allow dancers to use anything foreign in their pointe shoes because they want the dancer to "feel the floor" and toughen their toes, dancers have always found ways to protect their feet. A paper towel wrapped around the toes, for example, perhaps some tape and occasionally a bit of lambswool will work!

Lately, however, a range of commercial products have become available for dancers. Unlike the home-style "remedies" mentioned above, these are not bulky or obstructive and they actually help the dancer stave off injury.

- *Toe Wraps* by Gaynor Minden, used instead of surgical tape to wrap the toes.
- *Heel Grips* from Prima Soft secure the heels, keep the shoes from slipping off, and certainly save the tights when used instead of glue or rosin.
- *Pillows for Pointes* also help cushion the toes without losing the feel of the floor.
- *Flexers* from Primasoft, instead of elastic sewn into the ribbons, protect the achilles tendon.

The best cure for tired feet is a long soak with Epsom Salts at the end of a full day of rehearsals. Stock the house with lots of this old fashioned remedy for an appreciative young teen who has worked so hard through a day of rehearsals. Top it off with a little parental tender loving care!

The next step is breaking in the shoes. It isn't enough to customize them—now they must be molded to the young dancer's feet.

"What are you doing!" the mother exclaims as the dancer has stuck her new shoes in the door jamb and slams the door on them. "I paid a small fortune for those."

"I'm trying to soften the box." *Slam!*

Another mother might have an equal reaction as her young dancer fills her new pointe shoes with alcohol, swishes the liquid around, pours it out, slips the shoes on and walks around in them until they dry.

Or a father may seek his upholstery hammer, only to find his young dancer using it to whack against the pleating of her new pointe shoes.

"Are you insane?"

"They clunk and thud when they're new…" *Thwack!*

The techniques are as varied as the imaginations of the young dancers. The purpose? So the pointe shoe can become integral to the dancer's foot.

Of course, pointe shoes do not last long. A prima ballerina may use as many as three pairs in a single four-act performance of *Swan Lake* or *Sleeping Beauty*. A *corps de ballet* member will use one to two pairs in a week during heavy rehearsal and performance periods. An advanced dancer will use a pair every ten days or two weeks, and a young, beginning student can usually make a pair last for one to two months, perhaps even longer.

Even with all the new products now available, there remains a ritual for preparing the feet, getting the pointe shoe ready and putting it on.

First, surgical tape or *Toe Wraps* are wrapped around each toe separately to avoid rubbing and blisters. Then she wraps lambswool or paper towels around the toes and feet to further lessen the rubbing. But she will never wad lambswool or toweling inside the shoe first, as that will cause lumps and blisters. Some dancers use toe spacers to straighten the toes.

The young dancer makes a trip to the rosin box where her stockinged heel is immersed thoroughly, followed by a light dousing of water to insure the foot will not slip out of the pointe shoe (some creative dancers use a spot of commercial glue on the heel to do the same job). Perma Soft's *Heel Grips* also work well.

Next, the dancer slips the shoe on, crosses the ribbons over and around the ankle, and ties a neat knot beside the ankle bone. She would *never, ever* put the knot on the Achilles tendon! It should be tucked into the ribbon to avoid rubbing and chaffing and present a clean, sleek line.

When the young dancer is performing, she, herself, will sew the end of the ribbon knot to the ribbon so it will not loosen.

"So many things to remember," a mother might exclaim.

"My foot's no different than the rest of my body," the young dancer will reply. "The more beautiful my foot, the more beautiful my body. The more beautiful my body, the more beautiful my dancing."

The ideal female ballet body has a proportionate torso, long neck, small head and graceful arms. (photo by Jim Abel)

EIGHT

The ballet body

To most of us, special body types are meaningful only in the context of what is attractive or unattractive. "Look at that body!" a 19-year-old male might be heard to remark about a female counterpart, and we wouldn't have much trouble understanding his reference. "I love his body," a girl on the beach might say about a husky lifeguard, and there would be nods all around. Of course, we understand, *beautiful* is a body word.

So it is with the ballet body. The beautiful ballet body is not the same as the "beautiful body." "A beautiful body by society's standards" said says Robert Lindgren, "is not a beautiful body by ballet standards." What he means is that the ballet body must conform to certain special, narrow conditions that may or may not be appealing in the general public view. What he means also is that someone with a beautiful body would not qualify for ballet body praise. Ballet requires something different.

How different? Quite different—and the answer is elusive enough without adding the individual tastes and preferences of particular artistic directors who recognize the basic ballet body and then seek to remold it to suit their own artistic eye. Some place limits on height, others on body structure, still others seek a slightly more voluptuous form. It isn't that ballet's requirements are so varied; it is, rather, the individual needs of the artistic director.

Pacific Northwest Ballet's Francia Russell says, "I heard recently that we only like blondes, but that couldn't be further from the truth." She laughs. "I also heard that we insist on beautiful feet. Well, that is true. More to the point is that we look for malleable feet. Everyone looks at Patricia Miller's [a company prima ballerina] feet and oohs and ahhs, but actually she has one foot that is always photographed because it is so much better than the other one which was injured some years ago."

We can see the importance of the ballet body wherever ballet is performed. Over the past few decades a truly American look has emerged. The primary source for its development was George Balanchine, the late artistic director, founder and choreographer of the New York City Ballet Company. Balanchine—who was famous for his quote "Ballet is woman!"—had a love of long, leggy dancers who were very, very thin. Because of his influence, this body type became the standard by which the ballet body would be judged for many years, not only at New York City Ballet, but elsewhere.

Gone was the rounded female dancer of the late nineteenth to mid-twentieth century. First in America, and then world-wide, the changes developed, so that by the twenty-first century, the long, leggy, thin dancer was the look most directors sought. Other directors might have special requirements, such as height or form limitations, but the long-legged dancer became standard.

The current proper ballet body, based on the Balanchine influence and allowing for individual directors' variations, would resemble the following:

For women:
- a height of between 5' 2" and 5' 8"
- long, slender legs, straight and tapering
- small, flat buttocks and hips
- flat abdomen, small bust
- long, graceful neck and head, set perfectly on the shoulders
- soft, fluid hands and arms
- a strong well–defined back.

For men:

- a height of between 5' 8" and 6' 2"
- long, tapering legs
- strong feet and hands
- slender hips and waist
- strong, broad chest
- strong arms and shoulders
- strong, open back (to help execute the dynamic lifts)
- lithe, supple and flexible overall.

The ideal male ballet body should be strong,
well-toned and supple with good feet.
(photo by Angela Whitehill)

Like fashion, times and body styles change. What is proper form in one era may be unacceptable in another. Doris Hering, teacher and dance critic, and former director of Regional Dance America, says, "Probably the Balanchine influence will diminish as time goes on. Weight and body are a matter of style and fashion. I look at pictures of dancers in the mid-nineteenth century, and they look so fat to me, but that was the style in those days." The ballet body today should not be taken as an absolute for the decades to come. Over the last quarter-century, partly because of a greater understanding of eating disorders and the explosion of the exercise industry, we have seen a change in the ballet body. Now, the dancer is less likely to stress utmost thinness but more likely to strive to be a highly–tuned instrument. Dancers can better understand that a healthy body is one that has enough energy and tuning to withstand the rigorous days of rehearsals and performances.

The female and male body structure must complement each other in a pas de deux.
(Pamela Whitehill and Frank Della Polla) (photo by Bertha T. Kourey)

The dancer who might not fit snugly within the descriptions given on pages 58–59 should not feel discouraged. The American dancer is taller and more elongated than many of the dancers in Europe, and the requirements for the ballet body in Europe make allowance for this. Many shorter dancers who have trained in the United States go to Europe and find a ready place in a company. A male dancer who is six feet, four inches or a female dancer who is five feet should not assume that their bodies are inappropriate for ballet. They need to search long enough to find the proper fit. And it is true that there are artistic directors who see the sense of hiring smaller females, thus giving them a wider choice of men to lift them! One director in the northeast, whose choreography and repertoire were eclectic, had two principal females who were four feet, eleven inches and two who were five feet, ten inches; one of his male leads was five feet, four inches and another was six feet, five inches, and he used them all! In companies where there is a larger modern dance repertoire, it is not unusual for the women to be a little heavier as long as they are well–trained and well–tuned.

From the time I decided to become a dancer (at the age of eight), like every British hopeful, I had my heart set on joining the Royal Ballet in London. Nothing else would satisfy me, and I trained and trained with this in mind. One day, when I was twelve, I went to the studio to find that our teacher was measuring all of us. I had grown tremendously in the past year, and it unsettled me. Had I become too tall?

My worst fears were realized. I was now five feet, five inches and my company dreams were shattered. I would not be able to audition for them. Margot Fonteyn, prima ballerina assoluta of the Royal Ballet, was five feet, four inches, and it was common knowledge that no one was hired for the company if they were taller than she. Company policy, no exceptions. The prima ballerina could tower over the corps de ballet, but never, never could the company dancer tower over the prima!

Attaining the proper ballet body begins in the early years, because that is when good eating and exercise habits will become ingrained. Even at the ages of seven or eight, a knowledgeable director can choose someone with a potential ballet body. "I look for the good feet," says Marcia Dale Weary of the Central Pennsylvania Youth Ballet, adding that it is not useful to examine the entire leg too early because its form and shape will change with growth and training. "Maybe a slight hyperextension of the leg" could be examined, but foresight is limited. She looks for the way the child moves—the graceful neck, the turnout. Those are elements of the ballet body that will remain fairly constant as the child grows. But even at the Central Pennsylvania Youth Ballet young dancers always appear to be almost the same height and body–build on stage.

There is no doubt, too, that a director will look to the parents of a child to ascertain how the child might develop, for genes play a major part. So do the eating habits of a family. The eight-year-old child who comes into a studio with the "perfect" body and a family of overweight siblings is a director's nightmare. How does one explain to such parents that the child must develop healthy, careful eating habits early and continue through the teens to set his or her body habits for a successful dancing life, when the rest of the family obviously does not follow the necessary path?

Good teachers know how precarious it can be to make early, firm decisions about a child's body. Physical proportions change as the child grows. "Sometimes," related the late Lydia Joel, former head of the New York High School For the Performing Arts, "you get a little kid who looks like a dried mushroom but then begins to dance, and your heart goes out to her!"

There are few absolutes with the ballet body because tastes and styles are constantly evolving. The "perfection" of a generation ago is different from today's "perfection," which will be reconsidered a generation from now. The ballet body is, first, an expression of the art form and the instrument of the dancer, poised and ready to interpret the vision of the choreographer.

A dancer may be short or tall as
long as the proportions of the
body are correct.
(Pacific Northwest Ballet School)

A male dancer should have classes with a male teacher.
(photo by Cathy Vanover)

NINE

Special training for boys

The late Alexander Bennett, former director of the Scottish-American Ballet, told the story of his decision to learn ballet when he was seventeen years old. He was living in Leith, a small town in Scotland. "One afternoon I went to the King's Theatre in Edinburgh to see Sadlers Wells Ballet, and I fell in love with the prima ballerina, Margot Fonteyn." He felt a sense of joy and completeness he had never experienced before.

"I realized that this was what I had wanted to do all my life."

Then came reality. Dance ballet? "Where in Leith could I possibly find help? Male dancers were rare, to say the least, in my section of Scotland."

Rare, but necessary. For Bennett, and for countless other male dancers before him, the ballet world had an outsized need. Males have to perform certain movements that require substantial strength; males have to partner females in such a way that the grace and beauty of classical ballet could be demonstrated clearly, cleanly and harmoniously.

Unfortunately, a half-century ago, boys did not embrace classical ballet in the numbers or with the rush of enthusiasm that young girls did. But that has changed now, and as their numbers have increased, boys' ballet training has become more prevalent and more important.

Stanley Williams of the School of American Ballet, perhaps the foremost teacher of ballet for boys in the United States, acknowledges the more difficult, earlier days and describes why boys need special training. "It used to be harder for boys to dedicate themselves to ballet," he says, "and today that has all changed. It's acceptable for boys to be in ballet now. But they need to achieve enormous physical strength. Their success

"Line" and correct placement are essential to the well-trained dancer, both male and female.
(photo by Rob Martin)

comes from making feats of incredible strength look like nothing." Imagine today's lifts, *tours en l'air, grand jeté en manège.*

"The major difference between boys' and girls' training is style," says Arthur Leeth, former ballet master of Boston Ballet. "The arms and head movements are not so decorative." Grace versus brawn, beauty versus power.

For the first few years boys and girls should be taught together. They need to learn the same steps and general *ports-de-bras*; they need the same foundation. At about twelve years old, boys and girls at the larger professional schools are separated for certain classroom work. At the School of American Ballet, for example, boys now go to their own classes, and there they stay right through the rest of their training, joining the girls only for partnering and repertory classes. Smaller schools and particularly those in rural areas find it difficult to set up special classes for boys. But that should not prevent boys from receiving important training. It is perfectly appropriate for young boys to attend regular classes with girls, even in their mid-teens, as long as the special needs of the male dancer are met.

Pushups are the natural way for the male dancer to develop strength. (photo by Cathy Vanover)

However, please note that:

- The teacher must continually stress the need for development of strength.
- The male *ports-de-bras* (arm movements) should be developed to show strength and masculinity.

- A male teacher is preferable from twelve years on, and if one is not available, master classes taught by a male should be found for the young male dancer.

Tom Nicholson of North Texas Ballet Academy in Coppel (Texas) says, "Boys must move with more weight, from the way they walk to the way they assume their *ports-de-bras*. They must learn to be graceful and elegant without looking effeminate or like a peacock."

Although the male dancer needs whole body strength including a strong abdomen, the male torso and legs are in greatest need of strength. These areas receive the most pressure and use and must be fully developed in order to provide clean partnering techniques and bravura jumps, leaps and turns. To best develop this strength, Pilates training and cross training (using alternate forms of exercise to enhance the overall physique and increase performance) are the most effective methods because they offer special exercises and state-of-the-art machinery. The key is to develop long, strong muscles with good definition, not the bulky muscles of the weight lifter, which can interrupt the clean lines of the dancers' body and affect the grace and beauty of the art. Eddy Toussaint, former director of Ballet de Montreal, has his dancers do pushups regularly in order to build stamina and strength without developing thickened musculature. "Pushups" he feels, "are the natural way for muscles to develop," and he makes sure his male dancers stay away from weight lifting. He calls those who seek strength from weight lifting "over–developed."

Tom Nicholson has another point of view: "Modern resistance training offers numerous benefits if done correctly," he says. "Although male dancers generally have reasonable leg strength, the upper body is almost always overlooked until the boy reaches partnering age, at which time the panic sets in. Research indicates that for the adolescent boy, weight training does not greatly increase a pre-pubescent boy's mass, but it does give him a greater awareness of the use of his upper torso." He pauses for emphasis. "But the weight training must be supervised by a qualified trainer."

David Howard agrees. "Cross training is wonderful for the young male dancer. Ballet is anaerobic, so other training that gives the dancer an aerobic workout helps provide cardiovascular endurance," he says. "Pilates, too. I have seen young men open their backs with good Pilates training, more so than with any other method." Clearly, ballet class is no longer enough. In class a combination may last only a few minutes but a full length ballet lasts 40, 50 or 60 minutes or more. Endurance can be built by aerobic activities such as swimming, running, brisk walking, cross country skiing or cycling.

Cross-training also includes yoga, floor barre or T'ai Chi, which help the dancer's mind connect to alternate ways of approaching movement.

Pointe work is another area of training in which boys and girls are separated. For girls, going on pointe is the culmination of years of training; for boys the double *tour en l'air* and partnering are the rites of passage. Boys do not go on pointe nor do girls lift. But boys can, and sometimes do, take pointe classes to strengthen their feet. They wear regular dance shoes, and they follow the girls' exercises by going on *demi-pointe*, that is, raising themselves onto half-toe, to help develop their feet and ankles. It will give them added strength, and it will help them develop the long line of the leg and foot as one unit.

To Summarize

The purpose of separate training and classes for boys is to concentrate on those things boys must do within the ballet art: lifts, turns in the air, jumps and leaps and multiple *à la seconde* spins, movements that enhance the beauty and grace of the art form. Though the boy's emphasis on strength and stamina is far different from the girl's emphasis on delicate and breathtaking form, ultimately each must complement the other if true art is to result. Stanley Williams knows this, and that is why he says, "I can give class where there are both sexes in class, and I have to teach in such a way that each gets something he or she needs."

For boys the ballet reality is simple and straightforward: they are integral of the art form, and they have special needs that must be met. Those who have made a career from ballet understand this well.

Matthew Keefe didn't decide to become a ballet dancer until his late teens. "When I was in Chicago and undecided about a career, a fellow dancer sat me down and gave me the best advice I was ever given. He said, 'Go into ballet if you want to be a dancer. There are more ballet companies than modern companies, they are bigger, they have more money and need guys! You will always have a job as a well-trained ballet dancer!'"

A well-trained male dancer can find jobs with ease.
(photo by Paul Seaby)

By eight years of age, performing is part of the training in some schools.
(Vermont Conservatory of Ballet)

TEN

Performance and performing

Ballet, the performing art! Bruce Marks, former artistic director of the Boston Ballet, asks: "Why learn all those steps and variations if no one is ever going to see you perform them?"

A dancer does not have a product to sell or give, only the art that is within, trained and rehearsed, ready to perform for an audience. "I love to perform," say dancers in unison. To dance for oneself is not always why dancers learn to dance. They dance to perform, to show others that beauty and grace and story can emanate from stage to audience.

But dancers must *learn* to perform, they must *train* to understand the meaning and demands of performance. They must recognize that performing is to a dancer as a concert is to a musician. It is the way the artist communicates his or her art.

In some ballet schools performance is a part of the annual schedule. As with choosing the right teacher and right school (see Chapter Three), parents should carefully weigh the *quality* of the performances. And here, the spectrum is even broader than teaching styles.

Schools that offer recitals are the most difficult to assess because of the wide differences between their expectations of students. Parents should consider the following:

> *When do students start working on the annual recital?*
> Any earlier than two-thirds of the way through the school year means that too much time is being spent on a performance piece, and not enough is being spent learning technique.

How much time in each class is spent on recital work?

Fifteen minutes or more in an hour will jeopardize the technical skill of a young dancer. There should be extra rehearsals called if recital work needs more development.

How much of the recital is performed by the very young dancers?

Three and four-year-olds may be cute but they are not ready to be on stage. Performance is a gift given to those who study hard and have talent; in my opinion it is not the right of every child whose parent pays for class.

How much are you being asked to pay for costumes, shoes, makeup and tickets?

Recitals can be a part of the studio owner's business plan and be very lucrative. Costumes are often more than seventy-five dollars each (the more your child dances, the more dances they will be in), shoes range from fifty-dollars upwards: tap shoes, jazz shoes, modern sandals, flat ballet shoes and pointe shoes: one pair for each dance! Make–up artists and hairdressers add to the cost, as do the many copies of posed photographs you may have to buy.

What else might be possible? At Houston's American Academy of Dance, recitals are given every two years, and the entire school is involved. An evening extravaganza such as a "Cruise Around the World" might be offered where each class, and even the parents, are utilized in a story-like setting.

The following year becomes a "training year," with no recital, just good solid training. "Our performances are so much better this way and both our staff and parents can see the progress the dancers have made" says artistic director Angela Jackson. "We also have a non-profit Regional Dance America ballet company (see more on this in Chapter Fifteen). Dancers can aspire to this company, and auditions are held each year. The company is an honor company of the southwest region, and we raise funds to travel to and perform at the annual Festivals. We also produce a *Nutcracker* each year where company members dance the major roles, and children audition for roles as mice, soldiers or party children. Of course, we own the costumes for *Nutcracker* and use them year after year so parents don't have to buy them as they do for a recital."

At the Contemporary Dance Studio in Montpelier, Vermont, there is a recital every year, but it is low-key as far as costuming is concerned and very high powered with energy. The first act is always danced by the eight– to fourteen-year-olds (the six- to seven-year-olds don't perform) and the second act is performed by the studio's Teen Jazz Company and adult dancers. "This way the parents and children in the lower levels can see where they are going and what they are aiming for," says artistic director Lorraine Neal. "We don't have elaborate costumes, simply tights and leotards with an embellishment such as a scarf or belt or headdress." She points to the great emphasis placed on professional production. "It works! We sell out five performances a year, and the parents only buy tickets that they need. They don't have an allotted amount they must buy or sell."

At schools such as the The School of American Ballet in New York City and Westside Ballet School in Los Angeles, there is no annual or biannual performance, but the students perform in studio demonstrations. This enables the school to put full attention into the training of the young dancer, and it enables parents to see their children's progress.

PERFORMANCE VENUES

Where can a young dancer get solid, positive performing experience? The opportunities change as the dancer grows. The young child should only be seen in the studio setting. As they grow to eight or nine years old, amateur performances such as school talent shows, boy– or girl–scout demonstrations or, better still, a self–produced performance for grandparents in the garage or attic or with friends at a neighborhood picnic are all suitable showcases.

As children continue to grow there are a few summer programs that give the young dancer a chance to perform. At Burklyn Ballet Theatre, where we have a 500-seat theater, a huge professionally-constructed costume collection, lighting, sets and a full box office, we perform every week. Every week!

> *I was brought up in Great Britain where repertory theater is the way a young drama student learns his or her craft. During the summer months theaters all over the country offer high-quality performances that change each week. The young performers not only act in each show but they also help to make costumes and sets, layout the programs and even do a stint in the box office, all while rehearsing for next weeks' offering! Why not try that with dance, I thought?*

> *So I found a space in rural Vermont I knew was perfect. It was a large, empty barn with wooden floors and a high ceiling. A temporary stage could be built at one end and have the audience sit in the rest of it. A good place to experiment, I decided.*

> *"It won't work," I was told. "You can't put on a full ballet performance in a week! And where will the audiences come from?"*

> *They had a point, of course, and that first year we had one performance with only a single person in the audience. But it didn't*

matter; the dancers were thriving and loving the hard work. They still perform each week, in a real theater, sometimes to a full house. The dancers' ability grows by leaps and bounds. We send them back to their studios at the end of the summer tired, happy, their need to perform satiated for another year and with a renewed passion for their art.

Another wonderful performing opportunity is with one of the hundreds of companies that perform *Nutcracker* each Christmas season. This ballet affords parts for five– and six-year-olds as mice, and as the children grow older and taller, they become soldiers. When they become more proficient, they dance as party children or angels, and eventually they get to be lambs to shepherdess or take part in the waltz of the flowers. Then it's on to the snow *corps-de-ballet*! An ever-growing rite of passage!

Over the past ten years intensive ballet competitions have been growing across the United States and abroad. These should not be confused with the local competitions to which recital schools take groups of dancers where trophies are awarded to the schools. I feel that such competitions have little value to a serious dance student because they emphasize winning over the art of dance.

The most significant competitions—where the art of dance and the dancer are judged by an international panel—can become the most serious events in a young dancer's life. The most prestigious of these is The International Ballet Competition. This highly respected competition is held every year in a rotating venue: Russia, Japan, Bulgaria and the United States. It is where stars such as Mikhail Baryshnikov, Rudolph Nureyev and America's Amanda McKerrow have been discovered and catapulted to success with the greatest ballet companies in the world.

It is usually the final decision of the director or teacher whether to invest time and money to enter a dancer into national and international competition. The rehearsal periods are intense, the costumes must be of professional quality, and the demeanor and conduct of the dancer must be carefully honed to project beauty and grace as well as talent and respect. "There is a certain type of dancer who can withstand the rigors of competition" says Lisa Sheppard, artistic director of Gwinnett Ballet in Georgia. "I took a girl to the Premio Roma recently. She was just eighteen and she was the kind of dancer who is not easily upset. She had complete confidence in herself, she loved to perform and didn't let criticism fluster her. She was very versatile. You could put her on stage as Kitri (the gypsy dancer from *Don Quixote*) or as Juliet in *Romeo and Juliet*, and she was equally comfortable in either part and danced as though she *was* the character."

"I was amazed at the lack of respect of the dancers toward the master teachers in Rome," adds Sheppard. "There were wonderful masters teaching every day and only three or four dancers bothered to attend classes. Of course they were getting classes from their coaches but oh! the chance to be seen and to learn!"

A dancer must know what he or she is doing at a competition. Maura (not her real name) competed recently in a national youth competition in the Northeast. She did a beautiful job in competition but on the following day when a director of a major company was giving a master class, she didn't bother to attend. He asked where the girl was, because he wanted to see how she worked in class. He had hoped to talk to her about a possible job with his company! He surely will remember this lovely young woman if she goes to audition for him in the future, not because of the way she might dance or perform, but because she was the dancer he thought he might want to talk to about a contract with his company who never came to his class.

Competitions can be tough not only because of the considerable pressure to perform well, but because of the difference in stages, too. "In Rome the stage was outside, and they had built it out of huge sheets of plywood and painted it gray. It was such a strange surface that my dancer had problems turning, and as the week went by it became more and more slippery." In some countries the stages are raked or slanted towards the audience. At the International Ballet Competition, rehearsals run throughout the night and a young dancer can be scheduled to do his or her only rehearsal at four a.m. And often there are politics! Who gets the best rehearsal and performance time, who has to share time, who will follow whom, who will be allowed to observe; the drama goes on and on, the dancer running a gauntlet of egos.

The major competitions such as the Prix de Lausanne, The National Arts and Letters, The Princess Grace, the New York International Competitions and the Youth Grand Prix are good for the right dancers and they certainly are showcases for tomorrow's top dancers. But your dancer must be ready, *really* ready and possess a will of steel!

If he or she is going to take a partner, there are some important questions to answer at the beginning: is the partner also going to compete? Have the two dancers worked together before? Do they complement each other? Will their egos get in the way?

Then the focus is on the performance itself: what variations (dances) will they dance? Who will choreograph any new work? Who will design the costumes? Where will you find the headdresses? How much will the costumes cost (one professional tutu can cost up to $7,000!)? How many pairs of shoes will be used? How will you transport costumes and shoes to the competition?

Most successful contestants have had continuous, private, individual coaching well in advance of the competition, and it's best if the dancer's coach goes along for the duration of the competition. Once there, the rehearsals, classes and coaching must be carefully scheduled to maintain the dancer's calm and give him or her a chance to get the greatest benefit from the experience.

What are the benefits? Listen to David Howard, who has coached a number of international ballet competition winners: "The competitions are wonderful if the dancer is ready, coached, and prepared properly. They are great places for the dancer to be seen by directors from all over the world." Or to Amanda McKerrow, the first American dancer to win a gold medal in the International Ballet Competition in Varna, Bulgaria: "Ballet competitions are great if you go for the right reason. Like everything in life, it is more important why you do something than what you do, but I certainly couldn't have done it without the support of my family."

Amanda McKerrow (with Simon Dow) was the first
American dancer to win a Gold Medal at the
International Ballet Competition in Moscow, 1980.

The audition. (photo by Rob Martin)

ELEVEN

Auditions for the young dancer

A fact of life in the ballet world is that auditions are the way dancers are chosen. The process starts at a tender age and will be repeated periodically throughout training and into a professional career.

Usually, the first opportunity for a young dancer to audition is for the annual Christmas production of *Nutcracker*. Most versions of this popular favorite use children as soldiers, candy canes, party-goers, angels and reindeers. The story is this: a toy nutcracker is given to a young girl, Clara, and subsequently broken by her brother. In a dream, Clara's concern for the broken toy is rewarded by her magical "uncle" who takes the child through a Snow Forest to the Kingdom of Sweets. Here the "candies" from many countries dance for Clara, and the dream is brought to a climax by the dance of the Sugar Plum Fairy and her Cavalier.

Many companies use the same children for years. As the children grow, they are promoted to another role in the succeeding annual production, and the casts can be up to one hundred and more. Large, professional ballet companies give thirty or more performances during the holiday season, while the smaller companies may only perform a few times. For the larger companies such as Boston Ballet, Pacific Northwest Ballet and New York City Ballet, candidates for roles are easier to find because they can choose children from their own ballet schools. Auditions for roles in *Nutcracker* are held each year for students of local schools in open audition, regardless of whether the company is large or small. "How young we audition children for *Nutcracker* is different from how young they *should* be," admits Madeline Cantrella Culpo, artistic director of the Albany Berkshire Ballet Theatre, who is, nevertheless, resigned to reality. "They seem to sneak in at five years old, though we think six to eight is the bottom limit. Even so, some six-year-olds are not ready for auditioning or performing."

Alexander Bennett, director of the Scottish-American Ballet, would agree. For him a five-year old angel "doesn't take direction from heaven very well," and he didn't take a child for *Nutcracker* under seven. He held open auditions each year, though he liked to use dancers from his school. "We train our students in a way to understand our director's and choreographer's needs," he said, and this, of course, makes it easier to teach them their roles.

Since Boston has its own school of ballet, the audition process has a natural flow. All children must be studying in either the main or intensive programs and attending two classes per week. Children in the lower levels must have been in the school from the previous January, and those in the higher levels from the previous September. Although the company has no age limit, there are height requirements. The two-day audition process at Boston Ballet takes place in early October each year. The auditioners consist of the staff, including the artistic director, the children's choreographer and the wardrobe mistress. None of the teachers or principals from the school or its satellites are involved in the audition itself or in the selection process. Four casts are chosen, and each cast has an equal number of performances. At the end of the first day, the children are given a color which signifies their group. They audition again on the second day with their color group, and when the day ends, the four casts are set. Boston Ballet performs as many as sixty performances each season, so it is a big commitment, not only for the children but for the entire family.

What, though, do artistic directors and balletmasters/mistresses look for in young dancers? Certainly not being overweight, but of course there is more. "The children have to have a certain style," believes Madeline Cantrella Culpo. "They have to have very nice feet for their low or intermediate level of training. They should have a look of childhood innocence because *Nutcracker* is, after all, a period piece. The children should be graceful, and it helps if they have long hair." Or as Francia Russell of the Pacific Northwest Ballet says: "We look for good bodies. We love long legs, a compatibility with our company style, a facility to pick up combinations, and a good attitude."

The audition process carries with it the unfortunate possibility of rejection. Not everyone can have the role they wish; not everyone can perform to an artistic director's satisfaction. For a young dancer, even those as young as six or seven—the reality of rejection has to be faced. For some it will be a first experience, and every artistic director has seen sad faces, tear-filled eyes, quivering lips as someone else gets a coveted role. For the young dancer, the most sought-after role in *Nutcracker* is that of Clara, the child who shows concern for a broken toy and is rewarded with a fantastic dream, and it is in the auditions that this role is filled. "Clara embodies the spirit of Christmas," says one director. "She is most likely to be the child who can act, rather than the one with incredible technique. She must emanate a youthful innocence."

Each of the dancers lives with the possibility of rejection, whether they seek the role of Clara or another character in the ballet. At Boston Ballet parents are given an in-depth handbook which clearly spells out its expectations, both at the audition and during the performances, and how the parents can prepare the child in case of rejection. Over the past few years Boston Ballet and other schools and companies have become more conscious of a child's emotional ability to cope with rejection, and where they can, they try to soften the experience by talking to both children and parents in advance. Not infrequently, it is the parent, more than the child, who becomes upset at the rejection.

The rejection situation seems easier, somehow, with the youngest children. They come to understand that they will have their chance next year, or the year after that. It's in the next age group, eight– to ten-year-olds, children Madeline Cantrella Culpo calls "in-between" dancers, where problems tend to arise. She is gentle with the children, explaining that not everyone can be in the most sought–after roles, that there are other parts, and they should consider trying out for those. "We try to talk to them honestly, to make them understand this important experience, and to point out that we don't win at everything we do." Then she laughs as she remembers a recent conversation with two other dance teachers. They were discussing their own daughters and the *Nutcracker* experience. "Not one of them ever danced Clara," she says. "But they survived the experience."

Unfortunately, parents can get caught up in the rejection situation. It usually spells difficulty for the student, as well as for the relationship between student, parent and dance teacher. What the parents see and what the artistic director sees may be two entirely different performances, and it's best if parents stay away from the actual audition. In fact, most artistic directors keep their auditions closed in order to avoid unhappy consequences. Of course, parents and their children are interested in just one thing—why didn't the child get the role he or she auditioned for? Any competent artistic director would provide an appropriate answer. In most cases this suffices, but once in a while a parent cannot or will not accept the director's decision. The consequences for the child can be rather severe.

Madeline Cantrella Culpo remembers such a situation. One of her students danced Clara one year but had outgrown the role by the next year, though she still wanted to perform it. "The mother lived vicariously through her daughter—she had wanted to be a dancer—though her daughter was not blessed with a dancer's body. Whenever the girl did not get a part, her mother would try to force me to change my decision." This went on for years, and the daughter continued to be the pawn of her mother's ambition. Now, years later, the daughter is in her late teens. "She's suffering deep psychological distress, and she's no longer a dancer. Nor will she ever be a dancer."

Parents feel badly when their child is disappointed, when they see the tears in the child's eyes. Parents know that disappointment is a part of life, that it's perfectly normal not to win every time. Fortunately, the young mind is emotionally elastic, and a momentary disappointment often will be replaced with another interest—even a success—before very long. One dance teacher tells of a little girl who appeared at *Nutcracker* auditions for four years in a row without ever getting a part, until in the fifth year when she was chosen to become an angel. "She looked at it as a challenge to keep going," the teacher said, "not as an insurmountable rejection. Her mother did not complain once during those four years of rejection and now the girl is as happy as she can be."

AUDITIONING FOR SUMMER PROGRAMS

Equal to *Nutcracker* auditions in importance and availability for young dancers are opportunities in various summer programs. In substance and form, auditions for summer programs differ from *Nutcracker* auditions.

Summer programs, suitable for children over twelve years old, are usually from three to six weeks long. They are an intensive ballet experience that combine daily classes with rehearsal, seminars and some performing (see also Chapter Seventeen). Generally, auditions (which are actual one to two hour classes) are held for the programs between January and March each year (local ballet teachers can provide information about individual programs). Auditions are held in a number of locations throughout the country by the artistic director or school director of the ballet company sponsoring the summer program.

The children probably will not be familiar with the person conducting the audition. They will be less comfortable, certainly more nervous. Parents should recognize the signs and explain to the child that these auditions are similar to a master class in their own studio. The artistic director or school director has definite needs in mind: "We love a good attitude, a dancer who obviously loves to dance and wants to learn," says Francia Russell of Pacific Northwest Ballet. "We want our students to have a good and productive six weeks with us."

Audition classes for the summer programs can be quite large. Usually, each dancer is assigned a number, and the number is then matched to the application blank for attending a particular program. These resemble regular classes as much as possible, as the dancers are asked to do barre and center work. From this the auditioner can get a good idea, not only about the young dancer's technique and training, but also about his or her ability to learn combinations and choreography quickly.

It is a valuable experience to take these audition classes, even if there is no present intent to become part of the summer program. However, it is important to seek the approval of the person conducting the audition. Classes could become overcrowded and available spaces should go to those who are actually planning to attend if accepted. "I don't appreciate dancers taking my audition classes with no intention of coming to our summer program," says Francia Russell," unless they ask me first. Usually, I won't object."

Dancers are notified either at the end of the audition or by mail. Each program has a different system of notification. For example, during Burklyn Ballet Theatre auditions, the dancers rarely are told of acceptance or rejection at the end of the audition because of possible embarrassment in front of peers. By the end of the audition, directors usually decide who shall receive scholarships, and at Burklyn, who will be invited to join the company which performs abroad at the end of the summer season.

To use the Internet to find out about auditions for summer programs, go to a reliable search engine (such as www.google.com) and type in "summer dance programs." Also check the annual December and January issues of *Dancer, Pointe, Dance Teacher, Dance Spirit,* and *Dance Magazine* for dates and times. Plan to arrive at least thirty minutes early, fully prepared to take a one–and–one–half to two–hour class. There will be a nominal charge which helps defray the auditioner's travel expenses.

Parents should be aware that most dancers audition for many programs, and this is the correct thing to do. Often this means that space in the program may only become available as late as the beginning of June. It may not pay to wait that long. If the young dancer has his or her heart set on one particular program, it would be wise to audition early for just that program. If an audition is to be held in a neighboring town early in the season, make an effort to attend that early-season audition rather than wait for a later one that may be closer but already filled. For the young dancer, auditioning is experience, part of a learning process, and above all else, it should be treated as a master class.

An obsession with dancing, rehearsing and
performing is quite normal.
(photo by Carla Hunter)

TWELVE

Lifestyle of the teenage dancer

While other parents contend with the blasting cacophony of the current rage in heavy metal and rock, a young dancer's parents will hear the strains of Tchaikovsky, Stravinsky, or Vivaldi.

The young dancer will be dancing throughout the house, improvising ballets, rehearsing steps learned for an upcoming performance. Twirling, jumping with flailing legs, soaring arms, balancing a ballet foot on a recently cleaned kitchen counter. "I'm stretching. Dancers have to stretch!" High-kicking in the dining room. "You almost broke grandmother's china!"

The teenage dancer lives, eats and breathes dance. It is an obsession that quickly rise to excess. But this is not all bad! If the young dancer aspires to a career in dance, it's best to face this now. Dance is a way of life, it is a demanding and encompassing life choice, and teenagers with their single-minded obsession can begin to grasp what will be required.

In the morning, right out of bed, the young dancer will do thirty to forty minutes of stretching exercises, limbering up from the stiffness of a sound night's sleep. There may have been a late rehearsal the evening before, so unfinished homework must be faced. On the bedroom walls are posters or photos of ballet superstars—Mikhail Baryshnikov, Peter Martins, Ethan Steifel, Julie Kent, Amanda McKerrow, Paloma Herrera—role models, all. Pointe shoes litter the floor, some with ribbons severed or shanks pulled out, no longer usable. Sodden balls of lambswool fill a basket and bottles of floor wax or shellac share a table with polyurethane floor sealer and tubes and jars of theatrical make-up. Blue rubber *Therabands©* lie on the bed amid a pile of mutilated clothing.

"Is that the pretty leotard I bought you last month?" (The back has been cut and the front is safety–pinned. Full-length parachute pants have been cut into shorts.)

"It lets me dance better."

There's more. Tights have their feet and crotch cut out. "So I can wear them on my arms under a leotard," is the ready answer. Other tights have their foot bottom seams cut open, "so I can fix up my feet if they bleed or blister." In stark witness are bandage wrappers strewn about, some already opened.

Then there is the ballet bag. Made of lightweight waterproof nylon, it carries everything! Sweaty leotards, floor wax, deodorant, hairspray, crumbled cookies, an apple. Dig a little deeper and one will find four or five pairs of dance shoes (none in working shape), two tattered chiffon skirts, at least two pairs of flat ballet slippers, numerous pink and black tights, bobby pins, combs. Everything!

Ballet bag over a shoulder, homework under an arm, the young dancer now appears at the breakfast table—*and here is the parent's major responsibility.* In growing a fine dancer, a parent must ensure that the young dancer eats correctly, that a strong and healthy body is achieved and maintained. (For excellent advice on what dancers should eat, see *Diet For Dancers* by Robin D. Chmelar and Sally Fitt.) A dancer's body is his or her instrument, it must be kept at an optimum weight; strong growth without excess fat is crucial. This, of course, means that fast-food grazing and teen-diet crazes must be guarded against, that a balanced meal program is followed. (See Chapter Fourteen.)

It's not easy. "If teenage dancers would only care as much about what they put in their bodies as they care about what they put on their bodies, we would have much stronger performers," said the late Jeraldyne Blundin of the Dayton (Ohio) Contemporary Dance Company. There were eleven young people in her junior company who performed regularly throughout the year. Physically, it was a grueling schedule, especially when mixed with school requirements and teenage social demands. The dancers had to keep their bodies well-tuned. "I tell them that if they were musicians and playing a Stradivarius violin, they would polish it and polish it, would care for it completely and never let me touch it," she said, understanding, of course, that to demand such perfection from teenagers is highly unrealistic. "They don't yet see that they have only one body in one life, but…" Then she laughed, "They wear DKNY and eat at McDonald's."

Because dancers spend so much time in a very demanding physical activity, many parents find it important to ask if their child can be excused from physical education classes in school. Many schools will go along and schedule free periods during physical education time, or they will allow the young dancer to leave school early in order to attend ballet class.

But suppose a school doesn't want to—or can't—allow students to miss physical education classes? The first step for the parent is to investigate state education laws. Are there provisions for talented young people who wish to pursue a professional career immediately after high school? Some states do have such laws. They recognize that training during the school day, or training which duplicates school training and which leads to a professional career, fulfills state guidelines and therefore can excuse the young person from certain school requirements.

Are there performing arts programs in schools nearby? Some schools do have dance programs, and while they aren't designed to challenge the most skilled students, they do offer a viable alternative. Schools like these, bolstered with state funding, often waive the requirement of an audition and any student who wishes to dance is able to attend classes. One downside: the teacher, because this is a state education facility, will be required to have a degree in education rather than dance, and this may affect the quality of the dance instruction, though not the overall education experience.

The dedicated teenager dances everywhere.
(photo by N. James Whitehill, Jr.)

Performing arts high schools have been cropping up all over the country the past few years. In Brattleboro, Vermont, for example, a performing arts high school was created through the local vocational school, and dancers learn classical ballet as well as modern dance technique, technical production and dramatic presentation. Students can petition in ninth grade to attend the entire four years, unlike most voacational training in which attendance in only two of the four years is possible.

Another form of alternative schooling for the dancer might be the "magnet school," where there is a specialization in a particular area such as medical science, engineering or the arts. Magnet schools appear in and around most major urban areas. A serious dancer, looking for additional training and exposure, could benefit from the specialization these schools offer.

Understand the ballet demands on the young dancer—one–and–one–half hours of ballet technique class per day, a class in variations, modern dance, partnering, jazz dancing or character dancing once a week, plus two or three pointe classes per week. Many good ballet schools require their students to take classes in French, music notation and history of dance each week.

This adds up to a minimum of three hours a day, five days a week. If the young dancer is in rehearsal as well, a member of a junior or regional company, add another four to eight hours each week, plus some additional time as the performance date approaches.

Performing—it's what every young dancer wants to do, though sometimes such a narrow focus can miss other valuable aspects of the ballet world:

> *I was fifteen years old and a committed ballet dancer. I had left Canada with my parents' blessing and boarded a ship bound for England where I would continue my ballet studies. My vision was clear: in a few short years, I would become the toast of Europe, a ballerina with such grace and delicate movement that major companies would bid for my services.*
>
> *One day, as the ship plied its way across the Atlantic, I took a seat on deck and immediately noticed a woman wearing ballet shoes.*

"You must be a dancer," I said. She shook her head. "I'm a Labanotator." I had heard of Rudolf von Laban, of course. His work had been the major source of recording ballet choreography before film and video tape. His techniques provided a history of ballet choreography, and the system is invaluable.

But I was fifteen, and I was interested in performing!

"Would you like to learn dance notation?" the woman asked.

"Thank you," I said politely, "but I want to dance. I'm a performer, really.

Later, I found out the woman was Ann Hutchinson, a primary disciple of Laban, and in the week we were on the ship, she could have taught me the essential skills in notating choreography. But I was a performer. Period! My obsession didn't allow for anything else, including notation!

An obsession like this is quite normal with young dancers, and it shouldn't be cut off prematurely. If the obsession with dance can be encouraged and expanded to include other aspects of the dance experience, the dancer will benefit greatly. For example, knowledge of the history and the traditions of ballet are important for a full appreciation of the art form— watching videos of famous dancers performing both classical and contemporary work is not only inspiring but educational, as well. The young dancer needs to know the stories of famous ballets such as *Swan Lake* or *La Bayadère* so she understands what is expected of her on stage and how to convey their character to the audience. Performance tapes and books are readily available for the young dancer to learn the stories behind the roles they are chosen to portray.

Until the mid-twentieth century, there was no effective way to record ballets, they were simply passed on from one dancer to the next in the same way ancient storytellers passed on parables and legends from one generation to the next. A dwindling number of the early twentieth century dancers are still alive, and it's most instructive to sit at their feet and to listen to them speak of touring and performing with the grand companies such as Ballet Russes de Monte Carlo or London's Royal Ballet. Any young dancer who listens carefully should tingle at the sense of sheer artistry that her predecessors developed and at the foundation they provided for dancers today.

Of course, the key is for the young dancer to remain in place long enough to *get* the message, either to read it or hear it. Fourteen-years-old, glamour-obsessed, ready to fly off to class and rehearsal: "I've got too much stuff in my ballet bag, Mom, how can I cram a book or tape in there, too?"

The history and traditions of dance don't disappear, they continue to hover about the young dancer. In time, an appreciation for what's gone on before will make its mark. The young dancer will be grateful for the connection, unlike other teenagers who face steady peer pressure to use drugs, sex and alcohol. Dancers simply don't have time for these temptations as long as they wish to continue to dance. The peer pressure they experience will come from other dancers who are equally committed to ballet.

"I never had the temptation to be normal," says a twenty-year-old professional dancer who remembers her early teens. "My body was and is too important an instrument to put drugs and alcohol in it."

The lifestyle, then, of the teenage dancer is one of obsession and time constraint. There simply will never be enough time to do the things that friends and peers are doing, unless they, too, are dancers. Homework, school attendance, and social life will be greatly influenced by the demands of a dance schedule, and through it all, the young dancer must maintain a healthy body and a sound outlook!

It may seem as if dance has taken priority over every aspect of a young teenager's life, that nothing else will matter. Dance is simply one type of teenage obsession, as are computer games or rock music or pumping iron. The career demands of ballet may require utter dedication, but to the teenager there is nothing unusual about this.

Ballet is hard work and good fun, too.
(photo by Angela Whitehill)

Dance students at Interlochen School for the Arts.
(photo by Paul Heaton)

THIRTEEN

Performing arts schools

The late Lydia Joel, former head of dance at LaGuardia High School of the Performing Arts in New York City, told a story: "I remember talking with a teacher from Oregon who taught a literature class. Every April she asked the students to write an essay on spring, and the results were fairly predictable: 'the flowers are growing, the sun is shining.' Nothing creative or new. But one year something surprising happened. The music teacher joined her and they asked the students to look at spring as a musician would: how the wind blows, what it sounds like, how things grow…Suddenly, the essays on spring became vividly innovative, each completely different. One set a scene on top of the Empire State Building, another in a cave face to face with a hibernating bear." She laughed. "The point is that the students were unburdened from rote thinking. They were allowed to discover the limits of their literary selves."

Joel saw this literary exercise as the equivalent of what a dancer might experience in a performing arts school. "If a young person is interested in ballet as a career, it is far preferable to attend a performing arts school because dance and academics are taught side by side. One interacts with the other. The creative approach brings out responsiveness in all kids." It is the interaction of academics with dance, she believed, that fosters challenging and innovative approaches.

The performing arts school, unlike its cousin, the dance company school of ballet, was developed as a place where all the performing arts, music, theater, as well as dance, could be learned. It was a place where a young person with talent could remain at home and find training and performing outlets while maintaining a sufficient academic program.

The LaGuardia High School of the Performing Arts, developed in the late 1940s, was the first of its kind and achieved world-wide recognition from the movie and TV show "Fame." Well-known stars have graduated from this school, including singer-dancer Eartha Kitt, who was a member of the first graduating class. According to Lydia Joel, "the thing clicked like crazy." In succeeding years performing arts schools have sprung up elsewhere: Chicago Academy of the Arts, The Performing Arts School of Philadelphia, the Los Angeles County High School of the Arts and the School for Creative and Performing Arts in Cincinnati, all offering integrated dance instruction with academics.

More recently, magnet schools have been opening across the country. These public schools offer special education for gifted and talented young people, and were originally conceived to attract students of different racial backgrounds (hence the name "magnet"). Their philosophy takes into account that children don't all learn in the same way. If schools offer specialized methods of teaching and design special programs, geared toward their special interests, they would learn better.

There are various magnet schools specializing in science, language arts, mathematics and, of course, the performing arts. Most students who attend these schools also maintain their private ballet instruction outside the school. These schools can broaden the young ballet dancer's horizon. A student from Georgia states, "It helps me be more open to modern dance, which I didn't like. An up and coming challenge for me will be to choreograph a piece."

As with any other public high school, the performing arts and magnet schools are available to anyone residing in the community. Generally, auditions are required because the number of places in each class are limited—two hundred each, for example, in the four grades at the LaGuardia High School. Something more than desire, therefore, is required to get in, but not necessarily prior dance training. "What we looked for was a glow," said Lydia Joel, "a radiance, a sense of excitement and space, a presence. It's nice if it turns out to be someone who has had beautiful training, who has beautiful arches, and a gorgeous body. But training is not required. We wanted to see potential, something special."

The performing arts school is divided roughly into two parts: studio time and academics. Half the day is spent with one area, half with the other, though individual schools may put a little more emphasis on one segment or the other. There are few library or rest periods and no physical education in the dance related programs. The students are exposed instead to character dance, dance history, costuming or similarly related subjects that will broaden their exposure. The point of it all is simple—can the regular high school routine be reconstructed so that talented young people may pursue a career in the performing arts while simultaneously carrying on with academic requirements in the same place at the same time? After more than fifty years, the answer has to be a resounding yes!

"First, we must have a school," is the famous phrase uttered by George Balanchine, when the idea of the New York City Ballet was proposed many years ago. What he meant was that a ballet company could live best if it had a school to provide it with a continual flow of dancers who had learned *his* technique, *his* way. The school was—and is—the key.

How different can the school of a recognized ballet company be from a performing arts high school?

Actually, going to a company ballet school is the accepted procedure in most of Europe and Russia. A child is auditioned at eight or nine years old. Those who pass the audition are accepted into professional training schools where they complete ten years of ballet and academic training simultaneously. In Russia, for example, the young dancers graduate into the Kirov and Bolshoi Ballet companies; in England they move into the Royal Ballet or English National Ballet Company.

Watching the video *Children of Theatre Street* is a wonderful way to familiarize parents and young dancers with the training systems of other countries.

In Great Britain it is not unusual for a child as young as eight years old to go away from home to a boarding school. There are a number of schools that specialize in both dance and theater. At the famous Elmhurst (boarding) School for Dance, for instance, a child can choose to specialize in *Classical Ballet and the Performing Arts* or *Dance and the Performing Arts* as young as seven years old. Those choosing the ballet track must study all other forms of dance and also drama, music theory, and the Pilates method. Students have the option to take all the graded ballet Royal Academy of Dance examinations over the next five to seven years. Those choosing the *Dance* program are taught singing, musical theater and have the option of taking the Imperial Society of Dance's Modern, Tap and Ballet exams, thus preparing them for a career in musical theater. In 2004 Elmhurst will move to new facilities in Birmingham and become the core school for the Birmingham Royal Ballet.

In Hertfordshire, close to London, stands the pastoral estate "Tring," which serves as the lower school for the Arts Educational Schools in London, training dancers and actors in all aspects of theater (see Chapter Eighteen). The choices of curriculum are much the same as Elmhurst and the ballet dancers often graduate to the English National Ballet Company. All the British schools accept students from abroad. The cost, even including air fare, is considerably lower than sending a child to a similar school in the United States.

In the United States, the closest training approach to the Russian and European models is the School of American Ballet (known as SAB). Started in the 1950s by George Balanchine and Lincoln Kirstein, its graduates are groomed for the New York City Ballet (though not everyone is accepted). It is one of the finest training programs for the truly American dancer, although Pacific Northwest Ballet (in Seattle), Pittsburgh Ballet Theatre, the San Francisco and Atlanta Ballet Companies use similar systems. Over the years these schools have prepared dancers for careers not only in their own companies but with every major company in the world.

Unlike schools such as the Kirov and The Royal Ballet schools, the School of American Ballet is not state-supported. Everything is privately organized from funding to repertoire to performance schedule. SAB is a private ballet school. There are no academics, no high school classes—the concentration on ballet is even more rigorous. Acceptance is by audition and students apply from across the country. "What we look for first is the potential for training that body, "says Robert Lindgren, former head of SAB. "Good feet, high arches, limberness, a good proportion of the shoulders to the hips, length of neck, size of head…these are what we judge in the beginner." It is more or less the same at Pacific Northwest Ballet. "Long limbs, flexibility," says Francia Russell.

And if the young dancer has already had training? The answer is the same everywhere: no rolling feet, a decent fifth position, a decent *plié grand battement, pirouette,* a knowledge of the vocabulary and no bad habits!

If the young dancer is accepted into SAB, a whole new world beckons. The earliest age for acceptance is eight, and students can expect to take two classes a week. By the time they are sixteen or seventeen they will be required to attend ten classes a week.

During the early years, some children get a chance to audition and perform in the company's *Nutcracker.* Should the company require children in any of its other performances, the first place it looks is to the company school.

After years of training, which might include summer sessions, between thirty and forty dancers make it into the highest levels at SAB. From this group, dancers are chosen for the end of the year "workshop" which is attended by dance critics and company directors from all over the country. It is these dancers who have the best chance of getting a contract with a professional company, and it is from this elite group that the New York City Ballet is able to choose new company members.

SAB, Pacific Northwest Ballet, Atlanta and the San Francisco Ballet Schools offer no academic training. Pittsburgh Ballet Theatre does have an arrangement with the Schenley School for its dancers to attend high school, but since they do not have dormitory space, they arrange host homes. Living like this, however, can create problems, as a young dancer from Atlanta found out in New York City (before SAB had built dormitories). "The living situation was the most difficult problem to overcome," she says. "The school helped me find a place with a host family, but it just didn't work out well. I had difficulties with the people I was living with, and it wasn't a very good year."

There is still the matter of academics. For many children attending SAB the answer is the New York Professional Children's School (PCS), a private high school directly responsive to the time constraints and career orientations of the younger dancer. Actually, the student population consists of young actors, musicians, dancers and models, all of whom must mix training and performing with academic classroom time. "PCS is different from a regular high school" says Becky Metzger, who attended for several years. "In my Atlanta high school they didn't understand about performing requirements." That she might not be able to do a paper because she had ballet classes and rehearsals until 10 p.m. meant nothing. But at PCS it does. "The teachers are really supportive. It's small, maybe seven to ten in a class, and the school goes all the way through twelfth grade." What is important to the young dancer is this:

the school allows generous release time to attend dance classes, rehearsals, filmings and photo sessions. Students arrange their schooling around their career needs.

For young dancers who prefer to be trained outside New York, there is the North Carolina School of the Arts (NCSA) in Winston-Salem. It is the only state–supported school in the nation devoted exclusively to the performing arts, and its students live and train on the campus. The school gives the dancer a well-rounded education in all the arts, with an emphasis, of course, on dance. Dance opportunities abound: there are the annual *Nutcracker* performances, as well as other performances throughout the year in the school's fine theater. Sometimes dance tours of the state are arranged. NCSA, however, differs from a pure ballet school such as SAB or Pittsburgh Ballet Theatre. It looks to train dancers as well as other performing and technical artists, and the approach is more general. They are training for the field of theater and dance, not specifically ballet, and they do all forms of dance and theater side by side. The school also provides a complete college curriculum which, for some young dancers, can be daunting because they will be around students who are considerably older.

There are boarding schools in the US, the "preparatory school," which offer dance training on a par with an overall general academic curriculum. Among the longest established are:

St. Paul's School, in Concord (New Hampshire). The ballet program was conceived thirty years ago by Richard Rein, a former American Ballet Theatre dancer. Here, dance is treated as an extra-curricular subject. There is a separate building solely for dance, with huge, airy studios and several performing spaces. The school's emphasis is on academics, rather than the arts, and a young dancer seeking acceptance must satisfy the stringent academic requirements first. Once past this, an audition is required for the dance program. Scholarships are available.

Harid Conservatory, Boca Raton (Florida). Built in 1986 by an anonymous donor, this school has beautiful studios, elegant dormitories and fine teachers. Enrollment is limited and by audition only. Attendance in the prior summer's program is preferred but does not guarantee acceptance. Students are bussed to Spanish River (public) High School. All dancers are on partial or full scholarship with a dance clothing allowance for some.

Interlochen Arts Academy, Interlochen (Michigan) is probably the oldest pre-college arts school in America. Since 1962 the school has been home to all aspects of the arts. The ballet-based dance program takes only forty dancers, by audition, who study academics in the morning and dance from 1 p.m. to 6 p.m. daily. The dancers are exposed to all aspects of dance. The dance program's graduates are accepted into many professional companies throughout the United States. "However," says Sharon Randolph, head of the dance program, "last year we had a dancer who decided to go to college to study astrophysics!" There are no talent-based scholarships here, but financial aid is available.

Walnut Hill School, Natick (Massachusetts). The dance department was started in the early 1970s by Sydelle Gomberg. The program serves students from grades seven through twelve. Dancers are accepted into a ballet or modern dance major after audition. They take a minimum of two dance classes per day while maintaining a regular academic schedule.

The high school years are crucial for the young dancer. This is when the craft of ballet is honed or discarded. This is when a firm grasp of academics will or will not be attained. This is also a time when firm home values are learned. The parent who searches all avenues and develops good opportunities for their young dancer is the parent who is making an unparalleled contribution to a budding career.

Students at Elmhurst (England) School of Dance and Performing Arts.

Dancers are constantly aware of their bodies.
(photo by Rob Martin)

FOURTEEN

Proper weight and improper health habits

Too fat! Too fat! Too fat!...the young dancer's lament.

"I wish you'd eat better," an army of concerned mothers say, ruefully acknowledging an uphill battle. "You *need* your strength."

"I feel fine."

"You should have a healthy diet—you're still growing."

"Oh, Mother!"

So it goes. Legions of mothers and legions of young dancers have played this scene with appropriate variations through the years. The young dancer thinks she's too fat, the mother thinks she's neglecting her health in order to push her weight down.

The point with young dancers is this: they all—*all*—think they are too heavy; they all think they must lose weight in order to dance effectively and present the perfect body form. Weight loss, they think, is a magic key to ballet success.

Nothing could be further from the truth. Obviously, weight control—not weight loss—is crucial for a dancer. Grace and beauty are more effectively portrayed by a slim body than by a chubby one, but that doesn't mean a young dancer must strive to be lean at the expense of health and artistic expression.

The mother of a female dancer with a highly lauded international company told this story: "The artistic director recently choreographed a new *Nutcracker* and gave the solo role of Snow Queen to my daughter.

She was thrilled and determined to lose some weight before opening night—though the artistic director never suggested it. Ten pounds and a few weeks later, she had lost her strength and her muscle. A month before opening night she lost the part.

But I guess she learned a lesson. After tears and self-recriminations, she made up her mind to regain the part. Through careful and healthy eating, and with the loving concern and attention of the company's prima ballerina, she had put on enough weight so the artistic director allowed her to dance the part after all. And, in fact, she danced the part through the entire *Nutcracker* season."

A body at the proper weight performs with more ease and grace.
(photo by Dana Jenkins)

Is there a proper weight for ballet? Bodies come in all shapes, sizes and types. The perfect dancing weight for a five-feet seven-inch dancer can be as low as 110 pounds and as high as 130 pounds; for a five-feet two-inch dancer the proper weight can vary from 90 to 110 pounds. Body structure, muscle development, even bone size make the difference, and there simply isn't one answer for everyone.

That doesn't mean, of course, that young dancers won't think otherwise. In this—as in so many aspects of a dancer's training—the parent's role is to provide some form of equilibrium, some sanity to the young dancer's obsessive quest for pound shedding.

"Why not drink fruit juice?"

"Calories, Mom," a can of diet soda within reach.

Any juice, even plain water, would be better. The body is seeking liquid to quench the loss of fluid from sweat after physical exertion. Diet soda will accomplish this, but it adds nothing to the body's nutritional demands. The young dancer thinks that diet soda and perspiration are a trade-off, but that's not the case. When a dancer sweats, more than water escapes. Nutrients, such as potassium and sodium, must be replaced. Cranberry juice, even a low-calorie kind, will help more than a can of diet soda. And there is watermelon, too, because it's high in potassium.

"Weight is *my* problem!" the young dancer will insist.

"Your health is *my* concern!" the parent should respond.

Another bad weight control habit is smoking. Through the years dancers have used smoking to suppress their appetites. But there's always the risk that the cure will be worse than the disease. It has a double-barreled effect. First, smoking will cut into the dancer's ability to breathe, and this could influence stamina and strength, especially during extensive rehearsals and performances; second, it adds no nutritional benefit to replace the loss of weight the dancer seeks.

Pounds come off, perhaps, and with them whatever strength and physical development they represent.

People smoke for many reasons, and this book will not debate the morality of the habit. Parents should be on the lookout for one thing: does a young dancer use smoking as a way to control and/or lose weight? If so, then the parent should encourage a healthy, nutritional substitute so that lost strength and stamina can be replaced.

Concern about weight is important not only with dancers and their parents but also with school directors. Precise weight levels, however, are rarely followed. It is more a case of sensing significant change, noting a dancer "looks different" or dances differently. Few schools formally weigh their students, but many deal with weight informally. Teachers are on the lookout for marked weight gain or weight loss, and they will mention it right away if they see it. For most directors and teachers, the underlying concern is that the young dancer will panic about a sudden weight gain and go on a crash diet which may have serious physical side effects. Many of these young people are moving from puberty to maturity. Their bodies are undergoing change even without dietary pressure. The most difficult part is gaining and keeping energy, and as the young dancer's body grows, the last thing she/he should do is expend whatever energy she/he has by severe dieting. Usually, dancers put themselves through the agony of dieting because everyone looks so thin, and they want this look for themselves.

"I remember Gelsey Kirkland," says Amanda McKerrow. "How I idolized her. Whatever she did, I wanted to do—even trying anorexia and bulimia." She laughs. "I guess I just wasn't very good at either of those things, so I learned to eat in a healthy way to control my weight."

The fact is that the young dancer may be compromising her own natural growth patterns by dieting so strenuously. If you see weight loss, ask if it is caused by diet or a condition beyond the dancer's control. If it's diet–based, use other solutions such as finding an understanding nutritionist, therapist or physician specializing in these disorders.

Awareness by directors and teachers has helped us see the signs earlier than in the past. But these signs are not easily recognizable—the reddened middle finger—the clenched jaw are recognizable only to those of us who have watched dancers abuse themselves for years. Sometimes it's too late and hospitalization is required. Many dancers are obsessive and/or perfectionist. That is why in their own minds they are never thin enough.

One possible approach is that followed by the school of the Hartford (Connecticut) Ballet. Enid Lynn, director of the school, says that while they talk about proper weight, they avoid putting a great deal of emphasis on it. "We don't weigh students in, we've never done that. They know if they're overweight. All they have to do is look in the mirror. We also make it known to them that certain roles will not be available if their weight is too high or too low." If they are too thin, however, outside help is sought. "We talk to those we think are having trouble, and we recommend they get counseling. We know who to send them to, though we don't ride herd on them." Therapists familiar with anorexia, bulimia and other eating disorders are available, though the therapy is family-oriented. Their therapists, in fact, won't see the young dancer unless the family consents to come, too. The parents must see this not as a disease picked from the air like a common cold, but as something with roots that stretched back into early childhood.

"We always talk to the parents," Enid Lynn says, "but some don't recognize the weight loss problems their children have. After all, we see the young dancers undressed, so we know what's happening. Some parents, unfortunately, won't agree to participate in the counseling, so the kids don't get treated."

Listen to a mother who thought she knew her daughter. "When the director called to say she thought my daughter was anorexic, my immediate response was, 'Oh, no! She has a high metabolism, which we all have in our family. My husband and I are both thin, and our daughter eats well at home.' But, in fact, my child was anorexic. The food she was eating, we found out later, was pushed under napkins, into pockets, under her bed, always hidden. We were lucky that we were able to get help when we did."

Some parents and children are not so lucky—some dancers die from these diseases and others carry scars for life. Sadly, in these days of Internet access, the wrong kind of support can be found. For example, Internet chat rooms (one known as "The Secret Society of the Starving") offer a platform for anorexics and bulimics to exchange information and gain a new sense of identity and empowerment while ignoring the dangerous effects of their obsession. Help is available, though, with a recent book, *Diet for Dancers* by Robin D. Chmelar and Sally S. Fitt, who understand that dancers want to be both thin *and* healthy. Good eating habits are underscored; healthy, nutritious foods that dancers can consume without adding undue weight are described, and those items which offer poor substitutes for weight control are set out. *Dying to be Thin* is a frightening but informational video. It explains that eating disorders are not just found among athletes and dancers. It helps parents and their children recognize the signs and find help for the victims.

A well-understood path to the "perfect body" is exercise and cross-training, and once again the dancer in search of being thin, thin, thin, can be obsessive. Although there is no doubt that the pursuit of health and fitness, especially with Pilates-based workouts and equipment, can strengthen and enhance the dancer's body, overuse can have the reverse effect.

Because of constant dieting, over-exercise and sharp weight loss, many dancers experience irregular or absent menstrual periods. This results in a lowered level of estrogen, which will directly affect bone development.

Proper weight permits the body to perform in its most graceful, most sublime manner. Any young dancer who thinks of losing weight as the unlocking of a magic door to ballet success is bound for disappointment and heartache.

More than in any other aspect of a dancer's career, parental concern is crucial to the care and healthy feeding of a dancer. All of the dance-related publications *(Dance Magazine, Pointe, Dancer, Dance Teacher, Dance Spirit)* publish information on health issues for dancers. A talk with teachers, directors, even a professional dancer will help parents to understand the importance of their role.

Regional companies give young dancers a chance to perform in a professional atmosphere. The Roswell Dance Theatre is just one of the many companies which belong to Regional Dance America. (photo by Dana Jenkins)

FIFTEEN

The regional ballet experience

"Regional dance exposed me to the professional side of the art," says a young American dancer. In her early teens she met and studied with people the calibre of the late Robert Joffrey of the Joffrey Ballet and American School of Ballet, Barbara Weisberger of the Pennsylvania Ballet and the late Virginia Williams of the Boston Ballet. "I think I learned more about professional auditions in one forty-five minute seminar than anywhere else. And the classes and performances and meeting the other dancers was all wonderful."

The essence of regional ballet is an opportunity for a young dancer to test the waters of semi-professional ballet. Its public face is the annual festival where regional ballet companies come together for training, seminars and performances, and it is here that the young dancer can savor the fruits of grueling hours at the barre and late night rehearsals.

Its other face is providing high-quality community offerings in which young dancers have the opportunity to refine their art and to learn what it's like to be part of a dance company. Regional dance exists in most parts of the country, and the dancers perform on a regular basis throughout the year. Ballet teachers are aware of the regional company that is most appropriate and most convenient to their school. They can certainly offer recommendations and set up auditions. The important thing is to realize these opportunities exist, and young dancers should be encouraged to take advantage of them.

Dancers can become members of a regional ballet company at the age of thirteen, and frequently, they continue with the company right through high school until they enter college or go on to a fully professional career.

For the young dancer this means a commitment beyond what they have experienced up to now; it means they have become part of a close-knit group that will rely upon them to perform consistently and regularly. "We usually ask our young dancers to sign a 'moral' contract when they first join us," says Maxine Chapman, artistic director of the Vineland (New Jersey) Dance Company. "It isn't that we will take them to court if they break it, but that they understand they have agreed to a commitment, not only for themselves but to all the other dancers in the company." Chapman's company does twenty to thirty performances a year, offering both ballet and theater dancing (as in musicals such as *Cats*). "Our proximity to Atlantic City has given us the chance to get some of our dancers into shows and to perform on television."

A dancer joining a regional dance company must agree to make a one-year commitment to attend classes, rehearsals and performances. This is only fair, because company plans and programs often are set up at least one year in advance. In order to cast the ballets the artistic director will need to know which dancers will be available. It also represents the type of commitment professional ballet dancers assume, and the regional ballet company is a training ground for that elusive eventuality.

It is a major commitment for young dancers, and it should not be taken lightly. The average schedule includes a minimum of three one-and-one-half hour classes during the week, as well as four to eight hours of rehearsals during the weekend, often on Sunday. Parents should be aware that this schedule, coupled with the normal school schedule, can become burdensome unless the unabashed commitment is made. Dancers have to know that during these years, at least, dance will be the major focus of their lives. Anything less than a full commitment can only be destructive to the dancer, his or her parents and ultimately, the company.

For the conscientious young dancer the regional dance company can mean a permanent uplift in the dance experience. For mom and dad, it could mean that Sundays, Thanksgiving and the Christmas holiday season might be spent in a different manner, perhaps even a different location.

"The show must go on," the young dancer will offer without apology.

"Whatever happened to the holidays?" her mother and father will wonder.

"I love to dance," will be the reply.

The most important regional dance experience is through Regional Dance America, an umbrella organization that operates across the country. Started in the 1950s by Dorothy Alexander of Atlanta Ballet, Audrey Estee of Princeton (New Jersey) Ballet, Barbara Weisberger of Pennsylvania Ballet, Virginia Williams of Boston Ballet and Alexi Ramov of Lehigh (Pennsylvania) Ballet, Regional Dance America was designed to decentralize classical dance by spreading opportunities across the face of the country and to improve the quality of training for dancers and performances for audiences. The process was to offer annual dance festivals and to expose young dancers to new master teachers, new choreographers and choreography and to other dancers. Now, a half century later, Regional Dance America sponsors five festivals each year in separate regions of the country (northeast, southeast, southwest, Pacific and mid–west states), and they are the highlight of the regional company year.

As many as twenty-five to thirty regional dance companies appear at a festival, and the air is filled with teenage excitement, dance and performance opportunity. "Festivals serve to let the dancers see that there are kids from all over the country with the same commitment" said the late Jeraldyne Blunden, founder of the Dayton (Ohio) Contemporary Dance Company. All the dancers attend, even those who may not be performing, because it's important they see that many others share their interest, that they aren't alone. "It's hard for young dancers to withstand peer pressure from friends who aren't dancers," Blunden added. "'You've got to dance *again* tonight—why?' Regional dance shows them they have peers who *do* understand."

There's a lot more to gain from festivals than young dancers finding support from other dancers, of course. Maxine Chapman describes some of them: "Dancers get a chance to work with other dancers in master classes, to attend seminars, to perform on a national level with youngsters of the same age and to grow by watching other companies." It's peer learning carried out of the school room and into the dance world, and it works well. It can broaden a young dancer immeasurably. "Many of the 'classical company' dancers get their first glimpse of modern works at the festival performances," adds Chapman.

Festival performances are a showcase for young dancers. Summer program directors, as well as professional company directors, often attend and may offer scholarships, apprenticeships and even company contracts. "It's difficult to find this many young people in one place at one time all involved with the same thing," says the artistic director of a small professional company in New England. "We can usually find high-quality dancers here, whenever we need them."

For dancers in Regional Dance America companies, the dance year comprises four separate parts, and all company members participate:

- ballet technique classes, held about three hundred days a year,
- October through November rehearsals for *Nutcracker* performances,
- February through April rehearsals for the spring performance at home and the annual regional ballet festival,
- summer training classes at the National Choreographic Conference or July-August summer ballet programs.

The Craft of Choreography Conference, also sponsored by Regional Dance America, can be a most important experience for the young dancer because this is where she or he learns to step from thinking like a student dancer to the broader view of the professional. As well as performing, the young dancer now learns the basics of choreography. The choreographers use the dancers to create new works, and the dancers are expected to perform every day during the two–week conference. The dancers rarely work with members of their own company or with their own artistic director or choreographer, but they must do consistently high-quality work in class, in rehearsals and, finally, on the performance stage every evening.

"I believe that consistency is the earmark of the professional," said the late Jeraldyne Blunden, who regularly attended the conferences. After two weeks of intensive work with various choreographers, the student dancers would probably agree.

Not all young dancers intend to pursue a career in dance, but that should not prevent them from seeking to become a member of a regional ballet company. It can provide a young person with a full, active and healthy teenage experience. As Maxine Chapman puts it, "Regional ballet is like one enormous family. It's important that young people get the chance to perform in large, well-equipped theaters and before well-educated, appreciative audiences." The regional ballet experience, she emphasizes, is great for a teenager's sense of self-worth because it allows him or her "to dance and be applauded by their peers and nationally acclaimed teachers and directors."

Carla Hunter, parent of a young dancer in the Gwinnett (Georgia) Ballet, concurs: "The regional festivals introduced a whole new world to me. I realized, while watching classes, how smart these dancers had to be, to pick up the complicated combinations, often after being told only once! It certainly made me much more respectful of them and what they do!"

Alun Jones, former artistic director of Louisville (Kentucky) Ballet, underscores the value of the regional ballet experience for the young dancer: "They gain self-esteem which carries into their daily lives," he says. "But it also allows their directors to put students and the way they are being taught into perspective" as they are compared with dancers from many other areas and companies.

Further information can be found by visiting www.RDA.com.

The Roswell (Georgia) Dance Theatre. (photo by Haigwood Studio)

A foundation in ballet helps give a modern or jazz dancer
a clean line. (photo by Rob Martin)

SIXTEEN

Jazz and modern dance

Picture this: a fourteen year-old dancer with six years of ballet training taking classes two or three times a week with a total dedication to the ballet art form, when an audition is announced:

Young dancers needed for community-sponsored musical review.

The choreographer has Broadway credits, there will be payment and the possibility of television work.

"Not for me," the young ballet dancer announces.

"It's dancing," her mother responds.

"I'm a ballet dancer!"

"Wouldn't the experience be valuable?"

"But Mom! Ballet is art, the rest is just…"

"Is that what your teachers say?"

The young dancer blushes. "Not really."

A conversation like this is not uncommon in a young ballet dancer's home. But this dancer's attitude is really counter-productive. In their early teens, young dancers should have exposure to a variety of dance forms such as jazz and modern, folk and character dance. After years of classical ballet training, the young dancer should be ready for some variety. An exposure to jazz and/or modern dance training can create renewed interest in all dance forms as well as provide a previously undiscovered creative avenue.

A modern dance student at Pacific Northwest Ballet School.

Jazz and modern dance expand a ballet dancer's horizons because a number of career options now become available. Even if the young dancer is just thirteen or fourteen years old, opportunities for performing in musical theater, in television or films, in video or industrial productions requiring versatility are possible. A sound balletic training is the essential ingredient, and a young dancer with six to eight years of serious ballet work should not have difficulty performing jazz or modern dance choreography. Rochelle McReynolds, formerly of the Boston Ballet, started her career with ballet, but in her teens she found jazz dance more satisfying, and now it is her main concentration. "A large amount of work is available for jazz dancers," she says, "a lot of television work especially, if one pursues it. But dancers have to be willing to work in industrials (productions for commercial conferences that advertise a company or product), too. Generally, I could make more money with industrials than I could ever get shooting a commercial. We were seen by people who would eventually provide money to sponsor other performances." But, she insists, "Ballet is the basis." Ballet adds a clean line, the turn out and the extremely stretched foot so that line and arms are very clear in design.

Thelma had been trained in a well-known regional ballet company in the Middle West. She had beautiful ballet technique, and before she had finished high school, artistic directors from various companies were watching her with glee. Thelma accepted a scholarship to prepare to join a major New York City company, and her ballet career seemed poised at the brink of success. One day, she was offered a dance role in an industrial video to be shot in Italy utilizing not only her ballet training but her jazz work too. She accepted it and discovered how much she enjoyed the work. She gave up her ballet scholarship and devoted herself to commercial and video work across Europe and the United States. Two years later, Thelma was offered a part in the television series *Fame*. Once her run on that show was finished, she decided to go to acting school so she could become a full-time actress.

"She could have done anything she wanted," says the artistic director of that regional ballet company where she danced during her early teens. "From that base of classical ballet, which was her passion, she has really gone places."

Jazz and modern dance often are linked together by those who do not know dance, but actually they are quite different. "Jazz tends to work from the gut," says Rochelle McReynolds, "not that modern dance doesn't work from the gut, too, but it tends to be intellectual work from the gut, while jazz tends to be sensual from the gut." The pelvis is often the focus of work in jazz, while in modern dance the center of focus is more in the diaphragm. McReynolds continues: "the thrust of jazz dancing is much more sexual-sensual; the thrust of modern dance is much more intellectual."

In jazz technique the dancer learns to isolate each part of the body and then learns to change focus. Ballet trains a dancer to work all the sections of the body together, and when the dancer deals with jazz technique, she or he is able to understand the body isolations and to apply these isolations to today's choreography. Eddy Toussaint, former artistic director of Ballet de Montreal, describes the meld of ballet training and jazz application for his choreography this way: "It is still with beauty of line, beauty of pointe work, beauty of jump, but suddenly—là!—it is a jazz movement, something close to us, something the people can put in themselves." Jazz dance is us! It is earthy, it is basic, it is our physical selves in communication.

American modern dance was developed by forerunners Ruth St. Denis and Ted Shawn and their students Martha Graham, Doris Humphrey and Charles Weidman. Now there are many techniques and many approaches. Modern dance grew in the twentieth century with its own personal approach and with its own language. The vocabulary of classical ballet has had five centuries to develop and solidify. Modern dance is not so constrained, there is a freer style, more emphasis on interpretation. As Ruth Ambrose of Boston Conservatory says, "With classical ballet the emotion should fit the actual step, with modern dance the emotion makes the step."

Where, then, might one look for a good jazz or modern dance teacher?

Start with a good ballet school. Ask if the school teaches jazz or modern dance. If not, ask for a recommendation, *but be sure to insist that the recommended teacher bases his or her technique on classical ballet.*

Then, watch a class; examine the students carefully (they should not have bulky muscles such as one gets from aerobic training; the muscles should be long and lean). Find out about the teacher's *technique* (Graham, Ailey, Limón or Humphrey, for example); how much of the class is based on the technique, and in the case of modern dance, how much of the class is based on improvisation (too much emphasis on improvisation means that base technique will be undeveloped).

Jazz and modern dance expand a ballet dancer's horizon and repertoire.

Many dancers have their first introduction to modern dance in college. It is here, as Ruth Ambrose says, "The dancer has a chance to say something, and going to college gives the opportunity to spend four years in a nice confined space to experiment and develop technique and ideas." Modern dance rarely demands a certain type of body the way ballet does. Yet, stringent standards still need to be observed. The fact is that being overweight, with wide hips, tight joints and unstretched feet remains unacceptable, no matter the dance form. "Most modern dance companies do have ballet training side-by-side with modern training," adds Ambrose.

The same holds true for jazz dance, though once again, there is no such thing as the "perfect" jazz dance body. "Those with less than the ideal ballet body have more of a chance here," says Rochelle McReynolds, "though they still take ballet classes, too. When I look at a ballet dancer, I examine the extension of the line; when I look at a jazz dancer, I examine the same thing, but I'm more accepting. I search for texture rather than position. I try to find texture from beginning to end."

When I was seventeen, I enrolled at the Arts Educational Schools in London to continue my dance training. After years of ballet, I was upset to find we were required to take classes in all forms of dance, including tap. Such a come-down!

I did everything I could to avoid these classes but without success, and reluctantly I did what was expected. At the end of my first year, I signed up for an audition with Emile Litler Productions. They were presenting a musical Christmas show, and I was curious about the repertoire. To my surprise I discovered that the additional dance forms I had learned gave me an edge over other dancers who had only straight ballet training.

Yes, I got the job, and the lesson has stayed with me. For years, whenever I was on lay-off, I was always able to get a nightclub or musical theater job to tide me over.

If your dancer chooses to change from ballet to modern dance, look for a company whose repertoire includes work choreographed by such modern dance luminaries as Martha Graham, Alvin Ailey, Doris Humphrey or Lester Horton. Find out who will stage these works and where they were learned.

Most well-rounded summer programs offer modern dance, and it is here a young dancer may first dance in one of the major works. Floyd, a young dancer from Tennessee, is an example. He always thought he wanted to be a ballet dancer until he came to the Burklyn Ballet summer program. He started taking classes with Martha Graham School teacher Marianne Hrabi. After the first week he was hooked. A call to the Graham School in New York got him an audition, and after three months in the school, he joined the Graham Company.

The Ailey and Graham schools in New York also offer full summer programs, and it is during this time the young dancer, like Floyd, can discover a new aspect to his/her passion. If it's jazz dance the young dancer wants to do, the Gus Giordano School in Evanston (Illinois) is the foremost jazz institution in America, though, of course, there are other good schools that specialize in the form.

But just like looking for a good ballet school, you need to do the homework:

- Check the teacher's credentials (where and with whom did she or he study; how long has she or he been teaching?).
- Watch classes.
- Ask questions.
- Read about and understand the differences between classical ballet and other dance forms.

And remember these words from Alun Jones: "With good ballet training you can go into modern dance, jazz, musicals, even hip-hop. But not the other way around!"

Summer programs add a chance for exciting interaction with new friends.
(photo by Ashley Nemeth)

SEVENTEEN

Summer programs

"I really enjoyed the summer! I feel I accomplished a lot."

"This place is wonderful."

"It was a growing experience for me."

"I really love this program."

These reactions to one summer dance program mirror the feelings of many others in summer dance programs from one end of the country to the other. The truth is that, by and large, students and teachers have a good time in a well-managed summer dance program. Things are more flexible. There is less pressure, and new friends are made. Frequently, too, the program is located in a retreat-like setting far from crowds, noise and city temptations.

The learning can be strong. According to Francia Russell, director of Seattle's Pacific Northwest Ballet, which has its own summer program, the students "get exposure to the ballet idiom, to jazz, modern dance, character dancing and music appreciation. We want them to be productive."

The summer dance program world is not large, and those who have experienced it find an occasional surprise. Lisa, who danced with an international company, was in Italy a few years ago, performing and touring for an extended period. "One day, while I was rehearsing, I looked up to see a young woman in conversation with the ballet mistress. She was pointing at me, and the ballet mistress was nodding. All of a sudden it hit me! It was Joelle!—my roommate at the summer ballet program I had attended as a young teenager. 'Joelle?' I mouthed. 'Lisa!' she laughed. It had been six years since we had seen one another. After rehearsal we found out each of us was with a ballet company, and both of us were touring Italy!"

The summer ballet program should be approached a step at a time. First, ask the young dancer's teacher about which programs are available. Get an idea of which ones seem more suitable, more agreeable. Some programs such as Pacific Northwest Ballet actually spend an evening describing the most respected and serious programs to the parents of their students: which are safe, which offer performance opportunities, which techniques are offered. If, however, the teacher tries to downplay the importance of the summer dance experience and urges, instead, that the young dancer stay in his or her own studio for the summer, warning bells should ring. The teacher's interest may be more her own economic loss than have anything to do with the student's dance future. Teachers who don't encourage students to have a broadening experience, such as a summer dance program, may be unsure of their own teaching abilities.

Let's assume the summer dance experience is encouraged and promoted. What then?

- Make a list of questions concerning living conditions, training, food, locale, supervision, travel and recreation opportunities.
- The young dancer should talk with others who have attended summer programs, as well as with parents of those who have attended summer programs.
- Ask the director of the program for names of parents of former students who live nearby. Most parents are willing to share their experiences.

There are, in effect, five basic items a young dancer should consider:

- Are there performing opportunities?
- Is the setting rural or urban?
- Is there a company affiliation?

- Who are the master teachers?
- Who are the chaperones and counselors?

At Burklyn Ballet Theatre (Vermont) there are major performing opportunities at least once a week with a one-and one-half hour program, fully costumed and produced on a professional stage. But it is not the only way. Other programs prefer instead to concentrate on technique and instruction. The choice is an individual one.

The question of where the program is located can be important. Marcia Dale Weary, director of the Central Pennsylvania Youth Ballet, recommends that her students attend a summer program away from their usual environment. "As they get older," she says, "I think it's good for them. They see what it's really like to be in a summer school. They don't have regular school, so they don't have anything else to worry about, and they can concentrate on ballet."

A rural or urban school is really a matter of individual choice. The Pennsylvania Ballet keeps its summer program going in downtown Philadelphia, while the Atlanta Ballet boards students at a nearby university which can be reached from downtown by public transportation. Burklyn operates on a college campus in rural Vermont. What is most appealing to the young dancer is really the key, and for some, the summer program setting is crucial.

The company affiliation aspect of a summer program can be the most important consideration, especially if the young dancer is determined to join a specific company. Francia Russell of Pacific Northwest Ballet puts it succinctly: "If the dancer has decided that a certain company is the one in which she wants to work eventually, then stick with it." Join the company's summer program. Go back year after year.

Many major companies do have summer programs. The Boston Ballet, for instance, has two summer programs, one for those fourteen and over (which operates out of the ballet company studios) and the other for those on a professional track. As Bruce Wells, formerly associate director of the Boston Ballet, says: "The value of a summer program is allowing the child exposure to many different aspects of the dance medium. It's much more intensive, accelerated movement, and it puts the children into a position of deciding if they really want to become dancers."

In New York, the School of American Ballet (SAB) has a summer program, and of course, this could be one way for a young dancer to discover whether she or he might eventually seek a place with New York City Ballet. Regular, full-time students at SAB, on the other hand, are sometimes encouraged to look elsewhere during the summer. "Try a summer program in some other area of the country," the former SAB director Robert Lindgren told his students. "Aspire to the New York City Ballet. That's fine. But like a lot of things in life, once something can't be attained, you have to change, get your priorities in order and say 'my goals have now changed, too.'"

The non-company affiliated programs may not bring the young dancer into daily contact with particular company personnel, but that shouldn't create any less opportunity. At Burklyn, for example, master teachers have come from ballet companies across the country, and they are always looking for talented young dancers. Robert Barnett, former director of the Atlanta Ballet and long-time master teacher at Burklyn says that except for an audition in New York and one in Atlanta, he used to "look for company dancers while I guest [taught] in summer programs."

Company affiliated or non-affiliated, a summer program provides a young dancer with exposure to professional ballet teaching which *may* lead to further opportunity.

Most responsible directors don't take children under twelve because the training is intense (as many as three to five classes a day, and often five or six days a week) and the young child would tend to get overtired.

There are exceptions, though. At Burklyn dancers younger than twelve are accepted into a small intermediate program if they show unusual talent and have a teacher's recommendation. Even then, the school insists on a parent interview, and acceptance is gauged on whether an older brother or sister or another dancer from the same studio is coming, too. The parent is informed that acceptance is conditional, that if the child is not happy or does not seem to fit in, she or he will have to be sent home without a refund of fees. This is to make sure that parents and the young child understand the fragility of the decision.

> *At the age of six, I was sent to a boarding school that had no dance program. I was miserable and cried nightly. Six years later, at the age of twelve, I was given the chance to attend one of the finest boarding dance programs in Great Britain. My fear of being away from my family, based on the earlier experience, influenced my decision to refuse the new chance. Had I accepted, I would have studied with the Legat brothers, two of the finest ballet teachers ever to emigrate from Russia. No doubt my career would have benefited greatly from the training, and to this day I have deep regrets about my decision.*

For the child under twelve, the best approach is to search out a camp that may have some form of dance expression associated with it. There are a number of directories available in the local library which will describe these offerings and, of course, there is always the school guidance counselor. Look, too, in the Sunday *New York Times Magazine*. There is a camp directory that is kept current in almost every weekly issue. While these programs may teach a minimal amount of ballet, they offer arts and crafts, usually a number of sports and other recreation, and some provide an introduction to dance and theater arts. For the budding young dancer it is a way to continue an interest in dance while not being pressured to learn ballet movement that would be beyond his or her physical capabilities.

But once a dancer reaches the age of twelve, the summer dance experience awaits! Publications such as *Pointe, Dance Magazine, Dancer, Dance Teacher,* and *Dance Spirit* run advertisements from their December issues through the spring. These describe the summer programs and announce dates and locations for auditions. Because of magazine space limitations, however, the advertisements only touch briefly on what's offered, and the Internet has become a far better source of information. Simply click on one of the major search engines such as www.google.com type in "summer ballet programs," and read the results.

From January through March, summer programs audition dancers for scholarships (see Chapter Eleven for a complete discussion about auditions and scholarships). Scholarships range from complete tuition to minimal stipends which will, at the very least, reinforce the young dancer's self-esteem. Although auditions are not mandatory for acceptance in some programs, it does give the director a chance to see each young dancer, and there is always the chance that a scholarship might result. The auditions given by SAB and Boston Ballet are the most crowded because they offer many full-tuition scholarships. For the parent, the important thing to know is that since SAB is in New York City, the question of general supervision during the summer program need to be addressed. Despite the prestige of the SAB program, parents should ensure that their young dancers are well–chaperoned, fully–challenged, safe and involved throughout the day.

The benefits of a summer program are obvious, as the young dancer will have:
- New and different teachers and directors.
- New and different styles and syllabuses.
- New and different choreography.

- New locations and experiences.
- A possibility of either being referred for a job or getting into the company attached to the program.

Add to all this the chance for exciting interaction with new friends from other parts of the country and the social benefits that can result. "For children from out of town, just meeting other children who are doing the same thing can be pretty great," says Marcia Dale Weary of Central Pennsylvania Youth Ballet. "The children in my school are like a family. They visit each other almost as cousins, and their friendships last forever— sometimes they are forty years old and *still* have those same friends." In summer programs, the dancers are part of a group where almost everyone carries the same love and dedication toward the art form. They empathize with the desire to dance ten hours a day and perform every week. Students and directors form a bond that lasts and lasts. Here is what some artistic directors say about the summer experience:

> "We get regular phone calls and letters from former students seeking career advice."

> "We hear continually about former students' marriages, children, and unbreakable friendships with other former students."

> "We see former students at social engagements whenever we audition in their cities and towns."

> "We see our former dancers dancing in the major companies."

> "Now, we get e-mails from all over the world!"

Most summer program directors would say that experiences like these are common. Isn't it reassuring that dancers and directors can and do reach out to one another, no matter their age or corner of the earth?

In college dance departments, dance is an integral part of the students' daily classes. Students at the barre in the dance program at Brigham Young University in Provo, Utah. (photo by Mark A. Philbrick)

EIGHTEEN

The college dance alternative

Skidmore College, Oberlin College, Butler University, University of Louisville, the University of California at Irvine, Indiana University, the University of Utah and Boston Conservatory are a few of the many colleges and universities that have regular, professionally–oriented dance programs.

Is it a possible path to a dance career? Times have changed over the past years, but the lament about going through college, *first*, are often the same: "I'll be too old to have a career when I graduate!"

At New York's Juilliard School, where the dance division prepares its students for performing dance careers, students work with a variety of choreographers and company directors during their stay here. Graduates have gone into professional dance careers in such companies as Joffrey Ballet Company, Martha Graham, José Limón and Alvin Ailey Dance Companies and Hartford Ballet.

Molly Faulkner, who went to college straight out of high school, says: "At the University of Arizona I was dancing in the college ballet company, and that was the *only* place I was getting decent grades. I even failed English! I just wanted to dance." When she had an opportunity to join newly forming Ballet Arizona, she jumped at the chance and left the university. Later, she joined "Sesame Street, Live" as *Grover*, and she also danced with Disney, Japan. After three years on the road she was ready to return to college. She received a BFA (Bachelor of Fine Arts degree) from the University of Arizona, an MFA (Master of Fine Arts degree) from the University of Iowa and is currently writing her dissertation for a Ph.D. "I can't believe I failed freshman English," she says "I have always known I wanted to write about dance as well as teach! I simply wasn't ready."

Jennie Creer-King took a different direction. "The year I graduated from the University of Utah there were eight of us and we all had professional dance contracts," she says. The University of Utah Department of Ballet is closely affiliated with Ballet West, Salt Lake City's professional company. It also has it own company, Utah Ballet. To dance with Utah Ballet, dancers are invited from the fourth or fifth levels offered in the ballet department. But Jennie was chosen in her second year as an "aspirant" (similar to an apprentice) to join Ballet West and performed as a full company member while she got a BFA in dance.

"It was hard," she says. "I went to school at 7:30 for two hours each morning, and then on to company class and rehearsals from 10 a.m. to 6 p.m. and then back to evening classes."

Youth, of course, knows no limits! And drive is what makes a ballet dancer tick! But how do you decide which college to go to, what to look for and what will make the difference?

Again, the Internet is an amazing research tool, and it's a good place to start. Go to the Web site of the colleges you might consider. Examine the dance department faculty credentials. Have they had careers in dance? How many graduates are dancing professionally? How many classes in ballet, modern, and other forms of dance are students required to attend each week? Are there classes in other related subjects such as pedagogy, dance, theater and art history? What do the studios look like? What degrees are offered? Does the community support an orchestra, art galleries, a professional ballet or modern dance company, an opera, a theater company?

"Generally a conservatory program, such as the Boston Conservatory or Cincinnati Conservatory, offer technique classes and little core curriculum," says Molly Faulkner, drawing a distinction between a BFA program in which dancers can choose an emphasis such as modern or ballet but must also take all the core academic courses. Colleges that offer a BA do have more generalized programs with equal emphasis on dance and academics, and many of the better colleges and universities such as University of Utah and Indiana University have performing companies too. At Brigham Young University ballroom and folk dance majors are also available and students tour internationally with the school's company.

"A dance degree is one of the hardest to attain," adds Faulkner, "because dancers are juggling dance classes, rehearsals, performances and dance–related courses such as anatomy, kinesiology, notation, choreography production and arts administration along with all their academic courses."

In fact, it isn't much different than a dancer's frenetic schedule during high school years. Except, now, it's combined with dormitory life and doing laundry!

Those who attend college with a dance career still in mind have already put aside the incessant urge to give up everything *now!* To wrap themselves in a career *now!* They have made the choice that academics should not be dropped merely because they have reached seventeen or eighteen years of age. The thirst for knowledge lingers, and for many, it is the knowledge specifically related to dance. College may offer the opportunity to major in dance and minor in another field with a view to opening other career opportunities or in preparation for the day when a dancer retires from dancing.

In Great Britain things are different. "Young dancers in Britain try to get into companies or company training programs as soon as they leave school at about 17 or 18," said the late Alexander Bennett. "Some colleges, such as Edinburgh's Telford College, provide (technical) training from which students can expect to find dance-related work, but its more general dance—not ballet." Certainly the Arts Educational School in London prepares its students for all aspects of the dance and theater world. The curriculum includes all elements of dance and subjects related to the art including costuming, art and theater history, music, design and singing, but no core academics. Along with David Howard, Anne Hebard and Ben Stevenson, Bennett graduated from AES. They went on to careers dancing with ballet companies and musicals, choreographing, teaching and directing. The Rambert School in London offers a three-year Diploma Course and a One Year Advanced Certificate in contemporary dance. They have also had a close affiliation with Brunel University in West London. There are many excellent schools in and around London that prepare a young dancer for a job in a company. You may find out about them on www.danceeurope.net. An email to the school will bring prompt information including fees, which are considerably lower than in the US.

The committed ballet dancer in the United States knows long before college-age that she or he wants a career in ballet, and so tends to leave school and go into a company. Ballet companies are always looking for young people, and this adds to the pressure to try a professional career without college.

But if the ballet dancer (or his or her parents) insists on college, there are benefits. College dance programs are often the first chance a classically-trained dancer has to experience modern dance forms and dance history in depth. Many dancers in professional modern companies are those who studied ballet and then switched to modern dance in college. They may not have had the time or the chance to experience this dance form while in high school, and once exposed to its liberating and expressive approach they find themselves fitting their own style and training to the art form.

Choreography is another avenue that the dancer discovers in college or university. There are many opportunities to try classical ballet choreography and to experiment in the modern idiom. For the dancer who wants to choreograph, performing vehicles are essential. "In college you have the dancers, the department, the studios to rehearse in, the theater and production staff for performances and, of course you have the dancers," says Ruth Ambrose. "If you try to do these things independently, you have to rent a studio, find the dancers and hire a theater...it gets very difficult and expensive."

There is always the teaching alternative, of course. A dance career may include a dance *teaching* career, and to acquire these skills as well as unchallenged acceptability among educators, a degree is necessary. Colleges and a number of universities provide this training and offer a sufficiently rounded curriculum so that academics and dance training are interrelated. At Brigham Young University, for example, a five-year program in dance education is offered and graduates are certified by the state of Utah and able to teach in public high schools. The degree, by itself, doesn't make a dancer more acceptable to company directors, nor does it guarantee that one's level of dancing will be any more dramatic, fulfilling or expressive. What it does guarantee is that one's knowledge of the ballet art form—its history, its variations, its creation—is sufficient to teach others to appreciate the same things.

Suppose, now, that the decision to attend college has been made, and the major remaining question is *which* college. There is an appropriate dance program for everyone and there are ways to narrow the list so that a reasonable fit can be attained. First, find a copy of *Guide To Performing Arts Programs* by Muriel Topaz and Carol Everett (Princeton Review). You will find brief descriptions of every college and university program along with some information about curriculum and entrance requirements. There is also the *Dance Magazine College Guide,* published annually. Discuss your choices with school guidance counselors, visit each school's Web site. Once a list of acceptable schools has been made, visit the campus and do the following:

- Ask to participate in, or observe, several dance classes.
- Ask if the school requires auditions for acceptance or for placement (most auditions occur in the early spring but "drop–in" auditions can usually be arranged).
- Is the dance department within the fine and performing arts departments and are there separate ballet and modern departments?
- Seek out the theaters and performing spaces on campus.
- Ask if the dance department attends any of the national or regional college dance festivals.
- Ask if there is a performing company attached to the department and how many performances the students perform yearly.
- Discover whether the dance teaching majors have a chance to teach in local schools or studios.
- Find out where, and to whom, choreographic students show work.
- Seek out some of the dance majors and find out about their previous training and how demanding they find the program.
- Find out how the faculty is connected to professional companies and how many of the graduates find work in professional companies.

This last is important because having contact with companies can help a talented student secure a job right out of college.

And there are scholarships for dancers. Get a copy of *Music, Dance and Theater Scholarships* (Conway Green Publishing Company). Include your dance composite photographs along with your application. Though you may not get a scholarship as large as an equally–talented sports student, talented dancers are always an important addition to a dance program. "If you have already danced in college and are applying to a graduate program in dance, you should always get money," says Molly Faulkner. "The bigger the college or university's sports program, the more money there is in their fine arts program! There are fellowships, teaching and research assistantships. You just have to find the right fit!"

Jennie Creer-King has this to say: "You need professional performing experience before you go into a graduate program to really appreciate and utilize the learning. A terminal degree is one that will secure you a good teaching position in a college or university program where the serious dancer might attend. I know that I can give so much more to my students now than to some of the dancers I knew when I was doing my graduate work, because I have been there and done it all!"

What about a doctorate in dance?

Scholarships are available to well-trained dancers in college dance programs.

"I simply didn't know enough to become the teacher I wanted to be," says Molly Faulkner, on the cusp of receiving her doctorate in dance. "I had all the performing, the choreographic credits and knowledge, but I didn't have the introspection and thought process. I recently joined a small college in California where all the ballet teachers have had professional careers with major companies. The students looked at me askance at first, but once they began to take my classes, they understood that I really do know what I am doing!"

Intensity of interest, commitment to student progress, fine tuning of the ultimate career aspirations: all of these things vary with individual colleges or universities. But there is no doubt that a large performing, choreographing, and teaching field of opportunity exists for the young ballet dancer who has decided that a full time career now isn't what he or she wants. There are many dancers in professional companies nationwide with college degrees. "For many of these dancers," says an experienced artistic director, "the BFA or MFA programs become their company experience."

A dramatic resumé picture can come from a performance or a professional dance photograph session. (photo by Eduardo Platino)

NINETEEN

A full time dance career now?

It is in the last two years of high school, when seventeen and eighteen-year-old dancers are on the down slope of secondary education, on the verge of adulthood, that they have one more major dance decision to make. Teens huddle with parents…

Am I a dancer?

Do I want, and need, a college education?

The scene is replayed over and over across the country:

"I'll be too old to dance professionally if I go to college."

"Your father and I loved our college years."

"You weren't dancers."

"It's time to think seriously about your future."

"I am serious…"

After eight to ten years of class several times a week, and a continuing year–round dosage of ballet, the young dancer is not expressing a fanciful whim when she or he ponders the merits of pursuing a professional ballet career at the expense of a beckoning college education.

Take Becky Metzger, for example. At fifteen, she went to New York after being accepted by the School of American Ballet, and continued her academic education at New York's Professional Children's School. When she became eighteen, she had a hard choice to face—which wasn't made easier when the New York City Ballet offered her an apprenticeship contract. Some would have chucked further schooling to devote themselves totally to ballet. Not Becky. Instead, she applied to and was accepted by Barnard College in uptown Manhattan, while simultaneously agreeing to the NYCB apprenticeship contract. For a moment, she could pursue both options.

Not for long, however. Just a few months later, she was offered a company contract, and the dilemma presented itself anew. This time she chose differently. "I told Barnard I wasn't coming. I felt I should put all my energies into my dancing. I'll go to college one day, but not for awhile."

It is only right that a parent be concerned about a young dancer's continuing education. The ballet art form is not only demanding physically, but its opportunities are limited. And ballet does demand youth. During the early months in a company, a dancer hones the skills learned through the years and years of training. The physical demands are rigorous, frequent twelve-hour days, for example, while rehearsing for performances, plus daily ballet classes that sometimes run two or three hours each. When on tour, there is never enough time to sleep, eat, rehearse, do laundry or seek general relaxation. Performances come at a dizzying speed, and transportation from performance site to performance site can be at the most inconvenient times and in the most uncomfortable manner.

At eighteen, my son was undecided about his career. He had spent years backstage with me, learning the intricacies of technical direction. Should he join a ballet company or start college? He finally decided to enter college with a major in technical theater direction. The combination didn't work, and he changed to a full business major. Now he has a business degree and a skill beyond the limits of ballet technical direction. But...he's back with ballet as a production manager with American Ballet Theatre. "My previous training and experience helped me get this job," he says, "but it was the degree in business that sealed the contract."

Age, alone, does not necessarily tell a seventeen or eighteen-year-old that a ballet career may be lost forever if not pursued immediately. For some teenagers the years of training coupled with the limited opportunities may put the idea of a ballet career into the receding future, even though they have talent and desire. Impatience plays a part in this, as does constant comparison with peers: "Do I *really* have it? My extension is *never* high enough. My teachers have never believed in me..."

At the moment of the career dilemma, self-doubt flows through the young dancer's mind, unchecked and unappeased. The college alternative is certainly appropriate, but it should be chosen because the young dancer sees it as the next step on an affirmative career path and not because of an uncertainty that professional ballet will accept her unconditionally. Only with absolute certainty should the non-ballet alternative be followed. Anything less could sidetrack an ultimate ballet career.

Marcia Dale Weary, artistic director of the Central Pennsylvania Youth Ballet, tells a story that highlights how important it is to understand the clay that will mold the professional ballet dancer. "I had a little girl in my school who no one thought had talent. Her shoulders were too high, her extension was bad, her feet were poor. Person after person would ask, 'Why do you encourage her?' But this little girl loved ballet, and I could feel the desire in her. Nothing I could say or do would convince her to try something else. One day she came to class in a leg cast and insisted on trying to keep up, including the grand battements. So I started working with her, and gradually she got her extension up. She worked and worked on her turnout, she learned to hold her arms down so they had a better line to her shoulder, and she developed her feet so they were adequate, at least. Such desire!" Years later, it has paid off. "She's a lead dancer with a state ballet company now."

The career choice, then, is the product of many things, and talent may not be the most significant. Desire and determination play an important part, and the choice must be weighed with this in mind.

Is there a solution? Is there a win/win situation in which dancers and their parents can feel content?

Try this: during spring of the young dancer's eleventh grade year, plan to visit colleges where a variety of options might be available. Visit Butler University in Indiana, where the academics are high and the dance is good; or Skidmore College in Saratoga Springs, New York, where the young dancer can write her own creative program; Indiana University or the University of Utah where the dance departments are large and very diverse. Jeanette Buchner, who attended Indiana University after dancing with Oregon Ballet Theater, says "I loved Indiana and they have a great language program, but I guess what really sold me (on the school) was the opera house. It's as big as the Metropolitan Opera House in New York. I learned so much, not just in dance but in every aspect of theater."

Have your young dancer take the college's or university's ballet class as an audition for admission into the dance program; see how she or he fares.

Give your child the gift of a professional dance photograph session. This is not always easy, as you will need to find a photographer who really knows and understands dance. Ask the teacher or director of your child's ballet school for advice, or during *Nutcracker* ask the photographer who is shooting the performances to take specific photos of your dancer. Once you have photos, sit down with a magnifying glass and have your dancer choose the best photos. Then bow to your child's decision. A photo that you think brings out the beauty of your child may not necessarily be the one that shows his or her technique to its best advantage. Once you have chosen a few photographs, either make a composite sheet on your own computer or send them to a professional photographic house such as Modern Age in New York City and have fifty copies made.

Next, work with your child on putting a resumé together.

Professional photographs on a well-designed composite page, to accompany a resumé, are necessary for auditioning for a professional company.

During the summer after the eleventh grade year, have your child write the essays colleges require on their applications. Find out as much as possible about auditioning for a professional company in the vicinity of the colleges your child is interested in. Many summer programs offer advice and assistance to young dancers. For example, at Burklyn there are weekly seminars about where to find jobs, apprenticeships and traineeships. In addition, a professional photographer is brought in to photograph the participants.

Once your child's essays are finished, send in the applications <u>before</u> *Nutcracker* rehearsals start. Sometime before the end of the year, you will be notified about your application for early admission. If the news is good, send in the initial registration form and fee. Your child will then be enrolled in the college of his or her choice.

The next step is an audition videotape. Here the ballet teacher is absolutely key. Ask if he or she would be willing to help your child make a video. If you can't find a professional videographer, this is where dad can step in! Videotapes should be short, no more than ten minutes in length. Go to the Internet and check out what companies and summer programs specifically want to see of a dancer in an audition tape. The most usual requirements include barre work, center work, pointe work, and if you have really good footage of your dancer in a classical variation on stage, add that to the end of the tape.

Then, purchase or find at the library a copy of *The Dance Directory of Ballet Companies*. You may write for one at Post Office Box 904, Astoria Station, New York, New York 10023 (it costs less than $50.00). This lists most of the companies in the country. It profiles the artistic director and ballet master, lists the number of dancers, audition months and in some cases audition locations. It also provides the height of average company dancers, whether health insurance is offered, how many weeks contracts run and, in some cases, whether or not video auditions will be accepted.

There is no question that a personal audition is the best form of contact. During the late winter and early spring of senior year in high school a dancer should audition, audition, audition! "But that's so expensive," you might say. "Won't my child have to travel all over the country?" The answer is probably yes. Ask friends and family to donate frequent flyer miles and try to organize a single trip that will stop in as many cities as possible.

Then one day the phone will ring:

"Mom! I got a dancing job!"

"But, darling, what about college? You're already accepted."

"I'll defer!" is the triumphant reply.

Most schools will defer acceptance of admission for one or two years. Now everyone will be happy...for a while, at least!

Career or no career, college or no college, the dilemma faces parents and young dancers alike. A career in ballet remains a fragile choice throughout the young dancer's training years. There are always other alternatives. A commitment to dance, however, carries with it the focus of energies that can mold a young person into a positive, mature adult providing a joy to many others. For parents there has to be ultimate faith in the young dancer's vision of herself or himself.

Brigham Young University dancers are continuing their dance studies
and will receive a university degree, as well. (photo by Mark A. Philbrick)

TWENTY

You can do it all

Almost twenty years ago when the first edition of *The Parents Book of Ballet* was published, few dancers were dancing professionally *and* getting college degrees at the same time. The idea that a dancer could do both was a concept that simply hadn't been embraced by those in a position to act as role models for young dancers. Gradually, however, the idea took hold: a dancer could continue her professional career and acquire a college degree. At first, the numbers were quite small, but as the 1980s became the 1990s, young dancers found opportunities to combine their love of dancing with their determination to advance their education level. Today, of course, the idea that a dance career must be pursued to the exclusion of an on-going college education is no longer debatable; dancers can do both, and the following stories show some ways it can be done.

Rebecca was about to graduate from a prestigious preparatory school whose graduates are found in the finest colleges and universities. She was torn between a dance career and a college education. She wanted both and decided to pursue them together. She had her dance photographs taken by a well-known dance photographer, got her resumé in order and then applied to several colleges. By November of her senior year, she had been accepted at Brown University, her first college choice. Then she auditioned for various dance companies. She was offered apprenticeships with Nevada Ballet Theatre and American Repertory Theatre in Princeton (New Jersey) and she accepted the latter. She then called Brown and asked to be deferred for a year, and the college granted her wish.

During her first year with American Repertory Theatre, she made the role of the nurse in *Romeo and Juliet* her own. When her dance contract was renewed, she contacted the university and got a second deferral. But by the third year she knew college was what she really wanted, though she also knew she didn't want to stop dancing. During the spring season of that third year, Rebecca sought some help. "I still want to dance," she said, "and I need to know whether there are companies near where I'm going to school."

Rebecca (photo by Roy Round)

By coincidence, an audition announcement had arrived that day for a small ballet company in Providence (Rhode Island), where Brown is located. A call to the artistic director got Rebecca an audition—and a job. "It was hard work juggling college and dancing," Rebecca recalled, "but it was worth it for the first two years. During my junior year, I dropped out of the company because I needed to concentrate on my studies. But I still took class with the company to stay in shape."

On graduation, Rebecca moved to Boston and took a full-time position in the health-care industry. In her spare time she dances with Boston Dance Company which offers ten to fifteen performances a year.

"I have the best of both worlds," she says, "and I love it."

Matthew came to his dance career in a much different way. He was an economics major and a mediocre student in his sophomore year at the University of New Mexico, and dating a dancer. "She dared me to take a dance class based upon the Martha Graham technique," he recalled with a laugh. "Suddenly I found myself surrounded by pretty girls and learning things I never thought I could learn. It was an exhilarating experience! So much so that the next year I moved to Chicago to continue learning about dance."

He studied modern dance, jazz, and ballet at the Gus Giordano Studio in Evanston. He would clean the studio in exchange for classes, and

Matthew (photo by Paul Seaby)

came in early to have the studio all to himself. "Then I could practice the new steps I was learning."

After two years he joined the Lynda Martha Company, danced with the Chicago Lyric Opera and went to college at Loyola University part-time. "It was different now," he recalled. "The discipline I had learned in ballet classes helped to change the way I studied, and I finished the year with a 4.0 average!"

Over the next six years Matthew danced with the Fort Wayne (Indiana), Charleston (South Carolina) and Louisville (Kentucky) Ballet Companies, while spending each summer at Burklyn Ballet Theater. "It was at Burklyn in 1992 that I started to choreograph and each summer at least one of my works was staged there." In his third year at Burklyn he did an original ballet, *Cooking Sessions*. Alun Jones, former Artistic Director of Louisville Ballet Theatre, asked Matthew to set it on Louisville's junior company. The response was strong and the ballet was chosen for performance at the 1993 Southeast Regional Ballet Festival (SERBA). It won the Hobich-Corey Choreography Award, and "this gave me a scholarship to attend the Craft of Choreography Conference at the University of Iowa that summer."

During the conference, Matthew was asked by the director of the dance department to apply to the graduate dance program at the University of Iowa. He didn't have a bachelor's degree, but there was an alternative: he could substitute ten years of professional performance experience in order to qualify, and, fortuitously, he had just concluded his tenth year with Louisville Ballet Theatre. "I was accepted into the program, and two years later I graduated with a Master's degree. Now I could seek to teach and choreograph at the university level—but that was three years ago, and I still had some dancing to do." Since graduation, Matthew has danced two years with Ohio Ballet Theatre, one year with Ballet Met (Ohio), and most recently with James Sewell Dancers in

Minneapolis. He hasn't forgotten his university experience. "One day," he smiled, "I will use that M.A., and I'm sure glad I have it!"

Jeannette started still another way. She had trained with Oregon Ballet Theatre throughout her high school years. As graduation approached she received a scholarship from Georgetown University to study languages and linguistics. But the Artistic Director of Oregon Ballet Theatre also offered her an apprenticeship with the company. She had no doubt what she wanted to do. "All thoughts of college flew out of my head," she said. "I'm a dancer. I had the dance bug and it wasn't going to go away!"

Things went well for the first year, but in the middle of the second year she was injured. Recovery was long and arduous. Even with injury her contract was renewed for the third year. "I just wasn't feeling well and didn't know what to do. A friend suggested Indiana University because of its strong dance program. But I decided to go to New York and take classes and to...well, make my name in the dance world"

Jeannette (photo by Bruce Perkins)

She packed her car and started across the country, but on a whim she decided to stop in Bloomington, Indiana "Just to have a look! I loved it. After three days I decided to stay!" And stay she did until she had a degree.

"It was the best decision I ever made," she insisted. "While I was in college, I majored in ballet and German. I worked in the opera house and learned all about opera. I worked in costuming, makeup, on wigs and as a dresser. I met all the opera stars. I even did some lighting for modern dance and light opera. I got to go to every imaginable performance. I loved it." The university reciprocated: she was awarded the Leonard Bernstein Scholarship award for excellence in the arts. The entire experience made her the kind of dancer a director loves to work with—intelligent, informed and understanding of all that goes into making theater work well.

When she graduated, Jeannette came to Burklyn as a student counselor. It was obvious that first summer she was ready for a professional contract. She joined Charleston Ballet Theatre, where she has been dancing for the past three years. "Each year, parents ask me about college, and I tell them it was right for me. But it wouldn't have been right immediately after high school. I just wasn't ready and it would have been a waste of money. I don't think I would have received the Bernstein Award, either, if I hadn't gone right on to college."

Pamela provides one more way to "have it all." She went straight out of high school into a two-year apprenticeship with Hartford Ballet. Two years as a soloist with Ballet de Montreal followed, and then she went on to Omaha Ballet. While in Nebraska, she auditioned for the company of her dreams, Switzerland's Basel Ballet, under the direction of Heinz Spoerli—and she got a contract. But serious injury hit just two days later. After major surgery and a long rehabilitation, she finally decided her dancing would never reach its former level. With great sadness she turned down a position with a small company in the south and opened her own business called Kids 'N Motion; dance–related, but working with young children. It went well, but it wasn't satisfying enough to make up for her missed dance career. So, at the age of thirty, she enrolled in college.

Pamela (photo by Jim Thompson)

"It wasn't a hard decision for me at that point," she said. "I had come full circle and I was really ready to go to college. It was at the right time of my life. I think when you go to school at that age you are more likely to do well. It isn't a case of going to college because your parents say that's what you have to do. It's a case of going to college because you really want to go. Of course, the fact that you may be paying for it yourself really motivates you! I will always use my dance training whatever I do, I use it when I am teaching kindergarten class or simply playing with my daughter."

Rebecca, Matthew, Jeannette and Pamela each chose a different path to dance as well as achieving a college education. Their examples show that one choice doesn't rule out the other. With a bit of creative thinking, motivation and youthful exuberance, they could have it all!

And so can any other determined dancer.

BIBLIOGRAPHY

Ambrose, Kay. *Ballet Students Primer.* New York: Alfred A. Knopf, 1957.

_____ *Beginners, Please!* London: Adam & Charles Black, 1953.

_____ *Ballet Lovers Companion.* London: Adam & Charles Black, 1949.

Barringer, Janice & Sarah Schlesinger. *The Pointe Book: Shoes, Training and Technique,* revised ed. Hightstown, NJ: Dance Horizons/Princeton Book Company, 1998.

Buckroyd, Julia. *The Student Dancer.* London: Dance Books Ltd, 2000.

Cartwright, Hilary. *Dance As a Career.* Reading, England: Educational Explorers, 1974.

Chmelar, Robin D. & Sally S. Fitt. *Diet For Dancers: A Complete Guide to Nutrition and Weight Control.* Hightstown, NJ: Dance Horizons/Princeton Book Company, 1990.

Chujoy, Anatole. *Dance Encyclopedia.* New York: Simon & Schuster, 1968.

Cohen, Selma Jeanne. *Dance As a Theatre Art.* New York: Harper & Row, 1974.

Conway Green Publishing Co., *Music, Dance and Theater Scholarships.* South Euclid, OH: Conway Green Co., 1998.

Conyn, Cornelius. *Three Centuries of Ballet.* Sydney, Australia: Australasian Publishing Co., 1948.

De Mille, Agnes. *Dance to the Piper.* Boston: Little, Brown & Co., 1951.

De Mille, Agnes. *Speak to Me, Dance with Me.* Boston: Little, Brown & Co., 1973.

Elkind, David. *The Hurried Child.* Reading, MA: Addison Wesley, 1981.

Gallego, Liz. *Winning! The Dance Competition Handbook.* Dallas, TX: Self-published, 1999.

Geva, Tamara. *Split Seconds.* New York: Harper & Row, 1972.

Gilbert, Anne Green. *Creative Dance For All Ages.* Reston, VA: American Alliance For Health, Physical Education, Recreation and Dance, 1992.

Gordon, Suzanne. *Off Balance.* New York: Pantheon Books, 1972.

Greig, Valerie. *Inside Ballet Technique: Separating Fact from Fiction in Ballet Class.* Hightstown, NJ: Dance Horizons/Princeton Book Company, 1994.

Horosko, Marian & Judith Kupersmith, R.F., M.D. *The Dancer's Survival Manual.* New York: Harper & Row, 1987.

Hurford, Daphne. *The Right Moves—A Dancer's Training.* New York: Atlantic Monthly Press, 1987.

Jones, Mark W. *Dancer's Resource: The Guide to Workshops, Conferences, Artists' Colonies, and Academic Programs.* New York: Watson-Guptill Publications, 1999.

Kirslemann, John & Lavonne J. Dunne. *Nutrition Almanac.* New York: McGraw Hill, 1975.

Kirstein, Lincoln, Muriel Stewart, and Carlus Dyer. *The Classical Ballet.* New York: Alfred A. Knopf, 1973.

Krementz, Jill. *A Very Young Dancer.* New York: Alfred A. Knopf, 1976.

Lawson, Joan. *Teaching the Young Dancer.* New York: Theatre Arts Books, 1972.

Love, Paul. *Modern Dance Terminology.* Hightstown, NJ: Dance Horizons/Princeton Book Company, 1997.

Mara, Thalia. *1st, 2nd, 3rd and 4th Steps in Ballet.* Reprint. Hightstown, NJ: Dance Horizons/Princeton Book Company, 1987.

——————— *The Language of Ballet: A Dictionary.* Reprint. Hightstown, NJ: Dance Horizons/Princeton Book Company, 1987.

Mirault, Don. *Dancing…for a living—two.* Toluca Lake, CA: Rafter Publishing, 1998.

Phillips, Pat & Tom Armstrong, eds., *Music, Dance and Theater Scholarships.* 2d ed. South Euclid, OH.: Conway Green Publishing Co., 1998.

Sammarco, G. James, M.D. *Sports Medicine.* Philadelphia: W.B. Saunders Co., 1983.

Spilken, Terry L., MD. *The Dancer's Foot Book.* Hightstown, NJ: Dance Horizons/Princeton Book Company, 1990.

Terry, Walter. *On Pointe.* New York: Dodd, Mead & Co., 1963.

Topaz, Muriel & Carol Everett. *Guide to Performing Arts Programs.* New York: The Princeton Review, 2000.

Vaganova, Agrippina. *Basic Principles of Classical Ballet*. New York: Dover Publications, Inc., 1969.

Vincent, L.M. *Competing with the Sylph,* 2d ed. Hightstown, NJ: Dance Horizons/Princeton Book Company, 1989.

_____ *The Dancer's Book of Health*. Hightstown, NJ: Dance Horizons/Princeton Book Company, 1978.

PHOTOGRAPH CREDITS

Photos on pages 4, 6, 12, 19, 22, 28, 32, 33, 62, and 128 are used with permission of Pacific Northwest Ballet School, Seattle, Washington. Photography by Angela Sterling, Kurt Smith and David Cooper.

Photos on pages 44 and 152 are reprinted by permission of Gaynor Minden, Inc., New York.

The photo on page 72 is used through the courtesy of Vermont Conservatory of Ballet, Essex, Vermont.

The photo on page 100 is used with permission of Interlochen Center for the Arts, Interlochen, Michigan.

The photo on page 109 is used with permission of Elmhurst School of Dance and Performing Arts, Surrey, England.

Photos on pages 142 and 160 are used with permission of Mark A. Philbrick, University Photographer, Brigham Young University, Provo, Utah.

ABOUT THE AUTHORS

British-born **ANGELA WHITEHILL** began serious ballet training with the Canadian National Ballet before returning to the prestigious Arts Educational Schools in London. She danced professionally with English companies before joining Ballet de Paris in France. In the United States, she has served as artistic director, ballet mistress, costume designer, dance counselor and lecturer. In 1976 she created Burklyn Ballet Theatre, a summer dance experience in Vermont. Adding the Edinburgh Connection to the program in 1994, she has taken a group of young dancers each year to perform at the Edinburgh Festival Fringe.

Throughout the many years as artistic director of Burklyn, she has worked closely with parents of students, guiding young dancers on the path to professional careers. She led her own daughter through training and the audition process to professional positions with Hartford Ballet, Ballet de Montreal and The Omaha Ballet. Her son, also trained under her guidance, is Associate Production Manager of American Ballet Theatre.

WILLIAM NOBLE is the author or co-author of sixteen books, including *Bookbanning in America,* a nominee for the Eli Oboler Intellectual Freedom Award of the American Library Association, *How to Live with Other People's Children,* a Book-of-the-Month Club selection; and *Show, Don't Tell,* a main selection of the Writers Digest Book Club. His short works of fiction, as well as nonfiction, have appeared in publications including *Yankee* Magazine, *Adirondack Life,* the *Baltimore Sun* and *Newsday.* He is currently a contributing editor of *Garden State* magazine and has been a Vermont Humanities Scholar since 1989. His articles on dance have appeared in *Dance, Pointe* and *Dance Teacher* magazines. He is co-author, with Angela Whitehill, of *The Dancer's Book of Ballet* and *Ballet Magic.*

Ms. Whitehill and Mr. Noble are husband and wife.